What People Are Saying About
The 7 Best Things (Smart) Teens Do . . .

"I wish this book had been available to me and my parents when I was a teen. It's a treasure trove of psychological wisdom and guidance for today's teens and their parents. I highly recommend it."

William Doherty, Ph.D.
professor of family social science, University of Minnesota, and author of *Take Back Your Kids: Confident Parenting in Turbulent Times*

"In hindsight, my adolescence was marred by the extremes that both teachers and parents projected onto us teenagers, causing self-doubt and rigidity. Pity that the Friels were not publishing books when I was that confused teenager. Great work; keep it up."

Peter Charad
Bannockburn, Scotland

"Finally, a teen's guide to happiness and success! Destined to be a classic, this book teaches the wisdom of maturity with a genuine respect for youth. Required reading for teens, parents and all of those who have been either."

Pat Love, Ed.D.
author of *The Truth About Love*

"This book helps explain why it was all so difficult and why it needn't have been. I wish every parent could read it for their children and themselves. It's a second chance for all of us who have missed out on completing that second stage, to get through it and start to grow up."

Clare Trodden
Edinburgh, Scotland

"Few people question the fact that young people are challenges. However, many more would question the 'fact' that teenagers are challenges if they had the insights of Linda and John Friel. This book is must reading for both teens and parents. I especially liked the 'competence traps' and the 'tips' for teens."

Jon Carlson, Ph.D., Ed.D.
ABPP host of "Parenting with the Experts" and
distinguished professor at Governors State University

". . . the information is worthwhile, and if teens are motivated to read it, they just might find what they need to know to ease their life's journey."

School Library Journal

What Teens Are Saying About
The 7 Best Things (Smart) Teens Do . . .

"The messages in this book are so logically insightful that they seem like common sense. I readily identified with the inspirational intelligence this book has to offer."

Christopher Sheehy, 18
Dana Hills High School, California

"The 7 Best Things (Smart) Teens Do is a clear, easy-to-read book which will help teenagers better understand themselves and help them relate to their parents."

Liz Chu
Roseville High School, Minnesota

"Thank you for letting me read this wonderful book. *The 7 Best Things (Smart) Teens Do* should be required reading for high school health class."

Danny Suchy, 15
LaCrosse, Wisconsin, highest honor roll, varsity soccer and tennis, academic/athletic award recipient, Eagle Scout

"This book is funny at times, but also very serious. There is a great variety of stories and topics and a lot of great tips and advice. It is a very good book, and I highly recommend it to all ages."

John Giese, 18
Mora, Minnesota and freshman at St. Olaf College

"Drawing from many resources, this book successfully deals with the challenges every teenager faces and communicates a respectful understanding from an older generation."

Laura Wonch, 18
Grand Rapids, Michigan

Praise for John and Linda Friel's
The 7 Worst Things (Good) Parents Do . . .

"John C. Friel, Ph.D. and Linda D. Friel, M.A. have managed to write a witty, informative 'how-to' book on parenting. Distilling difficult—and sometimes controversial—subject matter into easy-to-understand concepts is not easy. However, the authors . . . cover everything from the mental anguish caused by well-meaning parents to the principles of Skinner's behaviorism, succinctly and completely."

Ruth Propper, Ph.D.
research fellow in cognition and neurophysiology,
Harvard Medical School

THE 7 BEST THINGS SMART TEENS DO

John C. Friel
Linda D. Friel

FALL RIVER PRESS

This 2008 edition published by Fall River Press
by arrangement with Health Communications, Inc.

Book design by Dawn Grove

ISBN-13: 978-1-4351-0602-4
ISBN-10: 1-4351-0602-4

Printed and bound in the United States of America

1   3   5   7   9   10   8   6   4   2

To all teenagers, their parents,
brothers and sisters, friends, teachers
and everyone else
who touches their lives

Other Books by the Authors

Adult Children: The Secrets of Dysfunctional Families

An Adult Child's Guide to What's "Normal"

The Grown-Up Man: Heroes, Healing, Honor,
Hurt, Hope

Rescuing Your Spirit

The Soul of Adulthood: Opening the Doors

The 7 Worst Things (Good) Parents Do

CONTENTS

PREFACE

In the Beginning

Let's work for a culture in which
the incisive intellect, the willing hands
and the happy heart are beloved.

—Mary Pipher, *Reviving Ophelia*, 1994

Fred Smith was once a student at Yale University in New Haven, Connecticut. He turned in a term paper outlining a business plan for an outlandish concept—to ship packages overnight from a central distribution point in Memphis, Tennessee. His professor thought it was very flawed and gave Fred Smith a poor grade on the paper, but that didn't stop Fred Smith. He went on to found the Federal Express Corporation—one of the most successful businesses in history. He must have had an incisive intellect.

Mother Teresa spent her entire adult life ministering to the sick and dying in the gutters of Calcutta, cleaning up

vomit and cooling feverish brows so that the people she
ministered to could die with dignity. She must have had
willing hands and a happy heart.

Mary Pipher offers us a poignant challenge.

This book was meant to give you something to think
about. It was designed to give you some facts and data
and theories and ideas that have helped a lot of other people get themselves successfully into adulthood. It was
designed to occasionally entertain you, and if it doesn't,
we apologize. It was designed to touch your heart. Above
all, it was designed to challenge and support you and
your family, all at the same time.

During the Free Speech Movement and the Vietnam
War protests of the 1960s, beloved San Francisco colum-
nist Herb Caen was as supportive of young people as anyone "over thirty" could possibly be. While there were
certainly aspects of the 1960s that were nothing more
than a generation of indulged kids with nothing better to
do than raise hell in public, there was nothing superficial
or narcissistic about the horrors of the Vietnam War, nor
about the Civil Rights Movement. There were real battles
going on, for real principles, that have had lasting, positive effects on American society. Herb Caen sensed that
there was something admirable and genuine about the
young people of the 1960s, and he wasn't afraid to write
about it. It felt good to have at least one "grown-up" on
our side.

Now it's the year 2000. As we put the finishing
touches on this little book, we want to assure you that
there are plenty of grown-ups on your side, and that
we have the utmost faith in your ability to grow up

yourselves and make the world a better place for yourselves and *your* children. We are both over the age of fifty now, and we're pulling for you!

ACKNOWLEDGMENTS

We would like to thank Peter Vegso, president of Health Communications, Inc., and Gary Seidler, now retired, for supporting our work for the past sixteen years. Having a publisher who believes that you have something worthwhile to say says it all. Peter and Gary, you're terrific.

We thank Matthew Diener, Lisa Drucker and Susan Tobias for their invaluable editorial assistance, and Kim Weiss and Maria Konicki for their tireless media support. Maria, you are a gem.

To James Maddock, Ph.D., University of Minnesota professor and clinical psychologist in private practice, for being our mentor since the early 1980s. It is an honor to be able to ask you for guidance and support. You continue to be a beacon of integrity and competence for us.

To all of our clients and ClearLife/Lifeworks Clinic participants with whom we have worked over the past twenty years, we thank you for putting your trust in us, and for doing the hard work that you have done to make your lives what you wanted them to be.

And finally, to our three children, for growing up to be such fine, competent adults.

WHY YOU SHOULD READ THIS BOOK

- You will meet the high school history teacher who got *everyone* in the class, including the "delinquents," enthralled with American history because he loved history and knew, above all, that teenagers love to think, challenge and be challenged.

- You will find out why adults who praise you for every little thing you do, but don't help you become competent at anything, are getting in your way.

- You will discover that *everybody of every age* has a hard time with feelings.

- You will learn how mastering your feelings is one of the most powerful things you can do.

- You will learn the difference between being powerful and being a victim or a perpetrator.

- You will learn how to get what you want without risking going to jail.

- You will find out that successful people fail, but they never quit.

- You will learn why "silently screaming" isn't nearly as helpful as sharing a personal secret or two with a trusted adult (and we'll give you some pointers about how to find an adult like that).

- You will learn the lifelong skill of identifying the extremes, such as why it is just as bad to be overly independent as it is to be helpless, clingy and whiny.

- You will learn why searching for what *you* want to do and be is absolutely *essential* for your later health, happiness and success.

- You will rest assured that sharing "the really serious stuff" is priceless.

Part I

The Agony and the Ecstasy, the Power and the Glory

1

The Parrot, the Appalachian Science Student, the Suburban Lawyer, the Media Rep, the Murderers and the Vandal, and the Grace in South Central L.A.

No plan is perfect. At any time we may have to abandon ship and jump into the unknown.

—Joan Borysenko, *A Woman's Journey to God: Finding the Feminine Path*, 1999

Out of Tension and Conflict, Respect

The Parrot and the Appalachian Science Student

A young man gets on a crosstown bus. He has spiked, multicolored hair that's green, purple and orange. His clothes are a tattered mix of leather rags. His legs are bare, and he's without shoes. His entire face and body are riddled with pierced jewelry, and his earrings are big, bright feathers. He sits down in the only vacant seat, directly across from an old man who just glares at him for the next ten miles. Finally, the young man becomes self-conscious and barks at the old man, "What are you looking at! Didn't you ever do anything wild when you were young?" Without missing a beat, the old man replies, "Yeah. Back when I was young and in the Navy, I got drunk in Singapore and had sex with a parrot. I thought maybe you were my son."

This joke has been circulating on the Internet for years, and is, in fact, so old and so corny that we should be embarrassed to pass it on to you. We aren't, however, because on further reflection it becomes obvious that we could design an entire university course based on sorting out the infinite levels of developmental and family dynamics contained within this fascinating little story.

Are there universal themes contained in this tale? Do all older adults feel this way about younger adults? Could there be a faint hint of warmth and playfulness in the old man's comment? If the younger man chooses to respond to the old man's sarcastic comment as if it might contain bits of warmth rather than just hostility, could the two men develop a friendship? Could their balanced confrontation—their squaring off as they did—allow them to attain a level of intimacy that is unimaginable had both of them sat silently in discomfort and contempt for each other? How is this scenario nearly identical to the poignant 1950s dynamic between Homer Hickam Jr. and his West Virginia coal-mining father in the autobiographical film *October Sky?* In that movie, the father remained angry, disappointed and distant for almost too long as his high school son, with equal stubbornness, pursued his seemingly impossible dream of building a successful model rocket and qualifying for the national science fair. Is there wisdom in humor, or only anger and contempt? Is strong conflict a key ingredient to the kind of deep relationships for which we all long?

Well, as we just said, it would be a piece of cake to design an entire university course around the themes and dynamics contained within this corny tale.

The Suburban Lawyer

"I think there ought to be a place to send kids when they're thirteen—a holding camp or workhouse of some sort—and then when they're twenty, they can come home." Thus spoke a successful suburban attorney who happened to be the next-door neighbor of one set of our parents a few decades ago. Was it angry and cruel? Judging from the care that he had for his teenage daughters, from their inner balance, and from the twinkle in his eye that accompanied the very real exasperation in his voice, we think not. Living in paradox and loving with depth go together, an idea that Confucius succinctly captured when he said, "Only the truly kind person knows how to love and how to hate."

The End Results of Growing Up—Or Not

Lynn Ponton, M.D., is the mother of two teenage girls, a professor of child and adolescent psychiatry at the University of California, San Francisco, and the author of *The Romance of Risk: Why Teenagers Do the Things They Do.* In a May 1999 commentary in *Newsweek,* she wrote that, "Keeping kids on the right track means maintaining parental involvement, encouraging them to take healthy risks instead of dangerous ones, listening instead of lecturing. Parents also have to watch their own risk-taking behavior—because teens are."[1]

Barbara Kantrowitz and Pat Wingert wrote that

In survey after survey, many kids—even those on the honor roll—say they feel increasingly alone and alienated, unable to connect with their parents, teachers and, sometimes, even classmates. They're desperate for guidance, and when they don't get what they need at home or in school, they cling to cliques or immerse themselves in a universe out of their parents' reach.[2]

And then there is this quote:

Our youth now love luxury. They have bad manners, contempt for authority, disrespect for older people. Children nowadays are tyrants. They no longer rise when their elders enter the room, they contradict their parents, chatter before company, gobble their food, and tyrannize their teachers.

[This passage is attributed to Socrates, who lived from 470 to 399 B.C. The more things change, the more they stay the same.]

The most common question asked of us by radio and television interviewers is: Do you think it is *harder* for kids to grow up nowadays than it has ever been? Our answer: It's *different.* After all, history tells us that in centuries past it was considered culturally acceptable and not the least bit unusual to beat, torture, mutilate and sexually abuse children. Even in this century, the plight of children in decades past had serious shortcomings.

In the 1950s when many moms were at home full-time, serious problems like child sexual abuse carried so much shame that even mental health professionals buried their heads in the sand. This left children to suffer silently and doomed them to carry their secrets into adulthood where they played them out with *their* children. Still wounded by the Great Depression and World War II, many parents wanted so badly to create the perfect suburban family life that they instead created a hollow external shell that masked all the depth and richness of being fully human. This eventually resulted in a nationwide revolt, from which we are still reeling in some ways.

Things may be confusing and difficult for parents and children right now, but surely current problems have solutions just like past ones did. In our work with families, we have found that the solutions to so many human problems are ultimately found by looking both at the extremes and at what constitutes depth with balance. When it comes to the goals of growing up, this approach is especially important. Kids want parents who have the guts to be parents, and kids want adults to whom they can look up, not away. We continue with a few more stories for your consideration.

The Media Rep

"I kicked their ass!" Sandra Hart gloated in April 1995. A renowned public relations executive, she had been picked up by the Minneapolis police who thought they had run across a "slumper," that is, a drunk driver who had pulled over in her car and fallen asleep or passed out. When her case came up before Judge Myron Greenberg, he regretfully dismissed it because of technicalities. Hart had a long history of alcohol-related driving arrests and convictions, but claimed that they had all occurred in the 1970s. Of course, the record showed otherwise. She had actually been arrested for drunk driving in 1981, 1983, 1984, 1988, twice in 1990, and again in 1993. When she commented on the judge's reluctant decision, she crowed, "I kicked their ass! I was never afraid or fearful. I had two things on my side: God and the justice system."

God is on her side? Is she out of her mind? The *Nazis* thought they had God on their side. The *Ku Klux Klan* thinks they have God on their side. *We* thought we had God on our side when we tried to carpet-bomb Vietnam into oblivion. Now this woman thinks that *she* has God on her side? When a parent slaps a child across the face and blackens his eye, the parent will often explain it by saying that he had to do it "for the child's own good." This may sound plausible to some people at first glance, but, of course, it is pitifully implausible. No research, experience or wisdom supports the goodness of such an act. We humans have a peculiar habit of believing that what we do must be right by the simple fact that we did it. We tend to be pretty narcissistic.

Another strange thing that many of us have a strong tendency to do is to actually pity—to feel sorry for and protect—people who do cruel, terrible things. At some level, we detect how damaged a person must be to treat others that way, and so the compassionate part of us tries to take over from the wise part of us.

When we recount the details of the above incident involving Sandra Hart to audiences of professionals who are attending a training seminar on working with victim-perpetrator dynamics, their immediate reaction is shock and disgust. As we interact more with the audience by asking questions and probing a bit beneath the surface, what everyone discovers is their inner reactions to things are not always the same as their surface reactions. For example, people who are angry with the law or with bureaucrats or with their parents or with the government may find themselves secretly applauding this woman's actions. People who are alcoholic or drug addicted—yes, there are psychologists, psychiatrists, social workers and counselors who are—may feel unconsciously protective of this woman because they share an addiction in common. People who were intimidated and hurt by abusive or neglectful parents may either find themselves wanting her crucified or wanting to protect her out of the symbolic fear of getting hurt again, or because of misdirected pity.

By way of an update, Sandra Hart was convicted of her *tenth* drunken-driving offense in December 1999 (shame on the State of Minnesota for letting it go this long), and she was finally sentenced to some jail time in January 2000.

The Grace in South Central L.A.

In 1990, Myrtle Faye Rumph's son was killed in a drive-by shooting. Within hours, friends and relatives had gathered to plan revenge. They watched and waited, put the neighborhood under surveillance, and planned to kill his killers. Myrtle Faye intervened, stating quietly that she didn't want to avenge her son's death, she wanted to memorialize his life. With no money and no government assistance, she set up the beginnings of a storefront teen center in his name. The center was to be a safe and supportive place for teens to congregate away from the violence and death that they experienced regularly. When she ran out of money, she sold her house and kept the center going. Five years later, her center had a yearly budget of $200,000, and had 125 teenagers gathering there on a daily basis. She summed it up when she said, "I didn't want to wait around for the city, the county or the state to give me the money to do it. It's up to black people to change our own destiny. That's what I'm trying to do."[3]

As the author of a *Los Angeles Times* article on Rumph

pointed out, Rumph "had an unlikely manner and scholastic background" for someone who wanted to start a teen center.[4] She had to drop out of high school in her junior year to help support her family, and later came to Los Angeles as a single mother with five dollars to her name. What a remarkable woman she must be. We have been reading her story to audiences since 1995. Each time we do, we have to hold back the tears in order to finish reading it. She is an awe-inspiring model for us and for everyone in our audience. We are especially grateful for a person like her because her wisdom is so profound and her humility so deep that we are forced to admit how far we have to go just to come close to her emotional and spiritual competence. Without people like her to remind us of how limited *and* limitless we are, we would certainly be lost. Myrtle Faye Rumph is one of the clearest examples of unmitigated power that we have encountered in the contemporary press. Her life is nothing less than an invitation for us to improve ourselves.

The Murderers and the Vandal

Lyle and Erik Menendez murdered their sleeping parents in cold blood a little after 10:00 P.M. on Sunday, August 20, 1989. During the shootings, which took a good deal of time, they ran out of ammunition. They had to run back to the car to reload their shotguns so that they could go back and finish off their mother, who was already bleeding to death from multiple gunshot wounds. Their first trial ended with the jury unable to reach a verdict because attorney Leslie Abramson had made such a convincing case of the fact that the brothers had endured terrible abuse at the hands of their father, and the brothers were therefore justified in killing their parents. They are now serving life sentences in prison because the judge in the last trial did not allow the presentation of their childhood histories.

Michael Faye, an American teenager living in Singapore, was caught vandalizing property. He was sentenced to the brutal, violent punishment of caning. At first, people in the United States were outraged, but when polled as to whether he should be caned or not, a majority of Americans said "Cane him!" Many Americans felt that caning was a barbaric, inhumane custom—it apparently turns the recipient's buttocks and legs into something akin to raw hamburger—but they seemed to be so impotently outraged at the lack of respect displayed by young people in the United States today that they were willing to let another country do their dirty work for them in this case.

Into the Power Zone

Is everybody a victim of something? Sure. Some of us are victims of war, terrorist bombings, child abuse or neglect, rape, beatings or other kinds of domestic violence. Certainly those of us who fall into those categories qualify as victims. Then there are the many of us who have suffered the ravages of hurricanes, earthquakes, tornadoes, floods or fires. It would certainly be reasonable to say that you were a victim of a terrible earthquake. Then there are terrible diseases that can strike anyone at any time, such as cancer, AIDS, neurological disorders and crippling diseases. If we had cancer, we could certainly say that we were victims of cancer.

But there's a difference between acknowledging that one is a victim of something on the one hand, and taking on the *victim role* on the other. To acknowledge that one is the victim of something is to acknowledge a part of our own reality, and it is therefore good for our souls do so. To take on the *role* of victim is another thing. To do that is to become helpless and powerless, and to blame everyone else for whatever difficulties we encounter. Being in the victim role means that we don't make decisions and we always have excuses why we can't do or try something. We react passively to life instead of actively engaging in the struggles that life sends our way.

For at least a decade, we have bemoaned the trend of Americans to confuse victim and perpetrator, and to somehow equate one *or* the other with being a mature, accountable adult. In our opinion, it is the simplistic black-and-white thinking considered normal in a five-year-old that accounts for this confusion. Five-year-old thinking in an adult body is a scary thought. Lyle and Erik Menendez undoubtedly suffered some kind of abuse or chemical imbalance, or both. Regardless of how the media sensationalizes tragedies like this by "going dumb" and ignoring the obvious, the simple fact is that people from healthy families don't go home and shoot each other.

The first jury in the Menendez brothers' trial apparently confused *why* someone perpetrates with *what consequences* should be meted out for the offense. Aside from organic brain damage, it is pretty safe to assume that most people who murder, rape, steal, batter or commit emotional violence were once victims of some kind of abuse or neglect in childhood. The solution to being a victim—the repair or fix for the painful aftermath of having been victimized—is not to become a perpetrator; nor is the fix for being a perpetrator to become a victim. The solution is to become an adult who is accountable. In other words, you face a choice: Do you act like Sandra Hart or like Myrtle Faye Rumph?

What of America's less than measured response to Michael Faye in Singapore? We adults fail our children by being absent, abusive or "pals" to our kids. When our kids display the resulting behaviors that one would expect from such lack of leadership, we become outraged and have extreme responses. What a mixed-up mess of motives, feelings and irresponsibility parents give their kids. Being a teenager has always been a challenge, but nowadays it seems at times as if it is a bigger challenge than ever because everybody—parents and teenagers alike—appear to be confused about this issue of personal accountability.

From Victim and Perpetrator to Powerful

The title of this book implies that there are some specific things that smart teenagers do. The stories and examples that we have used thus far were chosen to set the stage for the remainder of the book. They suggest that there is some inherent tension between teenagers and adults, which, if handled well, can result in unparalleled respect and understanding between them. They hint that there are certain ways in which adults are supposed to help adolescents move into adulthood. They demonstrate what happens when power is distorted and how confused we can all become when it comes to holding someone responsible. And then one story in particular shows the extraordinary things that happen when a person who has little reason to hope or care decides to take an incomprehensible risk, despite the wishes of everyone around her.

Human beings are imperfect by nature. Our flaws are what cause so much hurt in the world. They also are the very things that ultimately allow us to experience humility, which leads to gratitude, which in turn leads to the experience of grace, and then to the true holiness that springs from struggling with our own ordinary limitations. Mother Teresa said, "It is nothing extraordinary to be holy. Holiness is not the luxury of the few. Holiness is a simple duty for you and for me. We have been created for that."[5]

The struggle to pull ourselves out of the victim role and out of the perpetrator role is actually the struggle to become powerful. In *The Soul of Adulthood* we wrote that power without graciousness becomes perpetration, while graciousness without power gets us stuck in the victim role. The struggle to grow up and become truly powerful is not a challenge just for teenagers. It may manifest itself with special intensity during adolescence, but it is one of the universals that connects teenagers to middle-aged adults, old men and women to little children, infants to the terminally ill, and everyone in between to each other.

We chose this struggle to join grace and power as the centerpiece for this book because it captures all that is confused and painful about being a teenager today, all that is confused and painful about being a parent today, and all that is wondrous and holy about being human. *The Power Zone* is not a Pollyannish fantasy that is found only in self-help books. *The Power Zone* is a real, concrete and very attainable state that lies between being a victim and being a perpetrator. As has always been the case throughout human history, our struggle to discover and care for ourselves while discovering and caring for each other is the ultimate challenge and the ultimate high afforded to human beings.

Parents who remain vigilantly mindful that their teenagers are human beings, and teenagers who struggle to find the exhilaration that comes with combining grace and power, will each be rewarded, in the long run, with the respect and love that they each desire.

2

Thumb Your Nose at Gravity [6]

G reat spirits have always encountered violent
opposition from mediocre minds.

—Albert Einstein

American History X-Treme

"Memorize 125 dates and you'll get an A!"

"What did he say?"

"He said, 'Memorize 125 dates and you'll get an A.'"

"But that's . . ."

"Inane!"

"Did you just spell that word wrong?"

"No. I *meant* inane. But it was also insane."

When I was a high school sophomore, we had a history

teacher who didn't really know much about history: He was the football coach, and his contract required him to also teach something, so he taught history. You probably already get the picture. The class was world history. We had one of those textbooks that contained between its tattered covers a condensed and watered-down rendition of the entire history of the western world, from the Phoenicians, Macedonians and Egyptians of the pre-Christian Middle East all the way up to World War II! Yikes, David Letterman might exclaim! How could that be done? The answer: very tediously and with little depth.

Being the nonhistorian that he was, our teacher focused on dates in his exams. For our midterm exam, we had to memorize fifty to seventy dates, and for our *cumulative* final exam, we had to memorize those plus another fifty to seventy. I memorized 125 dates for that final exam, and I aced it. What a guy. What a waste. Years later—many years later, I should add—as I stood before the Tower of London with Linda, her mother and our three nearly grown children, I was able to say with great authority, "1066." They all looked at me, astonished. "The Battle of Hastings. 1066. William the Conqueror." They were *so* impressed. It wasn't until later that day that I shared with them the sordid truth—it was the *only date* from among the famous 125 that I still remembered.

At the beginning of my junior year in high school, I came face-to-face with the most interesting character in what we saw as our rogues' gallery of high school teachers. At first, this guy had us baffled. He was tall, thin, sort of pasty in appearance, dressed in tweed and seemingly shy. Most certainly, many of my classmates were licking their chops at the prospect of a new, inexperienced and vulnerable teacher they could slowly crucify for a year (it was a Catholic school, after all, so crucifixion seemed appropriate at the time).

He began to introduce himself and to explain how he planned to teach the course. He was a doctoral candidate in history. He loved history. His area of expertise was American history, and this was an American history class. Eager to make a splash right off the bat, one of my less restrained and more troublesome classmates jumped right in, raised his hand, and blurted out even before he was called on, "What about dates?! What about dates!?" The room fell silent. You could have heard a pin drop. All eyes were glued to the pale, thin face at the head of the class. Most of us knew that he was unaware of his predecessor's penchant for dates, and so our hearts stopped momentarily as a thoughtful gaze swept across his face. With an obvious love of history that was almost visceral in its intensity, he answered, *"Dates are the passion of the secondhand scholar!"* Instant pandemonium! It brought the house down! Questions and confusion quickly followed. What does that mean? How will we be graded? What will we be required to do?

He continued, animated now, "History is alive. It is a dynamic process of events and interactions among and between players, eras and cultures. It has multiple interpretations. There are thousands of ways to study it. You will need to know approximate time periods so that you have an understanding of the sequence of events, but it is *what happens in time, not the date itself, that is important.*"

Good God, we thought, *this guy is a pro.* By the time he was finished explaining his teaching philosophy and his view of history—which took the entire class—he had us chafing at the bit to begin what would be the hardest history class we had ever taken. We knew it and were excited about it anyway. The guy had magic! The guy had a brain! The way he was able to grab our attention was actually rather simple: The guy loved history.

What had happened to all of those date-anxious sixteen-year-olds on that warm fall Marin County afternoon in 1963? What happened was that this slight, shy, pale historian understood us. It didn't matter how. He connected with a bunch of sixteen-year-old boys and changed our lives forever because he understood us, he cared about whether we learned something or not, and he had a passion for history. He pretty much dispensed with the textbook and had us devouring original sources and tracing the crucial events of American history through the biographies of the men and women who *were* that history. He wasn't afraid to have us learn controversial things about these people, either.

He started with the story behind the myth of George Washington and the cherry tree. You probably know it, but in 1963 none of us did. Clergyman, author and bookseller Mason Locke Weems made up the story as part of his best-selling book celebrating our first president, *The Life of George Washington; with Curious Anecdotes, Equally Honorable to Himself and Exemplary to His Young Countrymen.* Everyone at the time pretty much knew that it was a celebratory myth. Then, as often happens as time slowly passes, the story took on a life of its own, until "one day," or so it seemed, every first-grade teacher in America was telling the story to children as if it were true. In fact, in 1963 a lot of elementary school teachers probably thought it was true.

Later, we learned that Benjamin Franklin had an illegitimate child, Abraham Lincoln suffered from serious depression, and Thomas Jefferson—considered by many to be among the top four presidents—had an ongoing affair and fathered children with one of his slaves. Was it relevant to us? Was it relevant to a classroom full of restless sixteen-year-old boys? Of course it was. This brilliant man knew that what Cicero said in 60 B.C. would be eternally true: "Not to know what happened before one was born is always to be a child." He knew that we were longing to flex our intellectual muscles, and he trusted that we were capable of doing so. He didn't *tell* us that directly because that wouldn't have been nearly as effective as challenging us and expecting us to be capable. At the end of that magical history class, this wonderful man said good-bye to a classroom full of educated students who would never be able to view history as boring again.

Teach Your Children Well

I tell that story every time I teach one of my graduate classes to schoolteachers in the Minneapolis/St. Paul area. I tell it somewhere in the beginning of the class, which is entitled "Working with Adults and Children from Dysfunctional Families." You might wonder why that story is relevant in such a class. To me it is one of the most relevant stories that I tell because, above all, the greatest gift that a teacher can give to a child who lives in a painful or even abusive family is *competence.* When I tell that story, I make sure to point out that when all is said and done, the kids who know something, and who know how to communicate it either in writing or by speaking, are the ones who will run the world. The rest will work at McDonald's. That is a bit of an exaggeration, but not much of one.

World-renowned anthropologist Margaret Mead said that she had nearly completed a book she was writing when the United States dropped the atomic bombs on Hiroshima and Nagasaki. She tore up the manuscript and threw it away, saying that the world had changed so drastically that the book was no longer relevant. The same sort of thing happened when Minnesotan Charles Lindbergh made his gravity-shattering solo flight across the Atlantic, when Neil Armstrong first set foot on the moon, and when the first pieces of the Berlin Wall came crashing down. In "Oysters and Pearls," Jimmy Buffett sang that Lindbergh "thumbed his nose at gravity," and that the world was forever changed.

Throughout history, we humans interpret certain events as so large, so influential and so powerful that we believe life will never be the same afterwards. We mark our brief stay on this planet by what we believe are transformative milestones. These include the Code of Hammurabi, the birth of Jesus Christ, Gutenberg's inventing the printing press, a solo flight across the Atlantic, harnessing the power of the atom, the first lunar landing, the first genetically engineered cure for a disease. . . . What will be next? You probably know better than we do what that might be, to be honest.

Rebellion or Transformation?

Some people call the time when a child is twenty-four to thirty-six months old the "terrible twos," which I have always found to be so interesting. In fact, upon the birth of my first child, I was given the well-intentioned advice to "enjoy them when they're little, because the older they get, the harder they are to raise." Even in all of the inexperience of my youthful new parenthood, a voice inside of me said, "That doesn't make any sense." I turned out to be right. There are always at least two ways to look at the same events. When that first child became two, all I could think was, "What a wonderful age to be!" I watched her strive to be independent. I listened to her say "no!" and by so doing, she declared to the whole world that she discovered she was separate from us. Terrible twos? No, it was the wonderful twos.

According to Jean Piaget, easily the most influential developmental psychologist in history, the years from thirteen to nineteen are transformational in just the same way. Many adolescents (unfortunately not all) will gradually shift from what he called concrete operational thinking to formal operations, which includes, among others, the ability to truly hypothesize—to ask "What if?"—the ability to think systematically and to test out hypotheses systematically instead of impulsively and haphazardly, and the ability to empathize with others at a much deeper level.

Part of this transformation is the crucial need to question and wonder, and especially to question many of the values and beliefs that we were given in childhood. In other words, not only is it normal, it is also *essential* for teenagers to ask things like: "Is there really a God?" "Can a truly good person feel hatred?" "Is the universe infinite, or is it finite?" "Does two plus two *always* equal four?" "Can I be a wise person and vote for a political candidate for whom my parents would surely never vote?" "Did Thomas Jefferson really father children with one of his slaves?"

Parents who recognize this emerging autonomous thought as a sign that their teenagers are healthy, normal and "right on schedule" will rejoice and feel relief, even if they find their adolescent's challenges exasperating at times. Parents who don't understand that this is healthy and normal may find themselves anxious about it, which may cause them to try to control or even prevent this exciting milestone, resulting in unfortunate consequences.

I am fifty-three years old. I grew up in the 1950s and 1960s in a suburban home about twenty-five minutes north of San Francisco. My older brother and sister and I watched the early black-and-white television programs pretty regularly after we bought our first TV set when I was five or so. We watched many of them with our parents, who were as enthralled with this new technology as we were, if not more so. My father and older brother watched the *Friday Night Fights* and the whole family watched *Your Hit Parade,* waiting in breathless anticipation to see what songs or instrumental pieces were picked as the top ten of the week.

As silly as it may sound now, one of my disappointments during grammar school was that our family was unable to watch the *Mickey Mouse Club.* We lived at the base of some coastal mountains with a bunch of redwood trees just up the hill, and our reception for that channel was nonexistent. I'd go to school the day after it showed and listen to my close friends talk excitedly about what had happened on the show, and I tried to follow along, but something was obviously missing from my experience. You had to see the show to appreciate what they were talking about, I gathered. Regardless, it was part of the culture in the 1950s, and so it was important.

Barry Levinson's film *Avalon* (1990) is a celebration of his own family history as well as a testament to the enormous, irreversible impact of both television and "suburbanization" on the American family. When I first saw the film, I finally realized, in a visceral way, how profoundly these two cultural forces had affected all of us back then. As my father, mother, brother, sister and I huddled around that little television set in 1954 waiting to see which song would be number one on the hit parade, we didn't have an inkling of how our lives were being transformed. Few people could have predicted the multitude of transformations that little tube would go through, and all of us right along with it.

The historical and cultural contexts in which we grow up have a huge impact on how we turn out. Developmental theorist Erik Erikson, who formulated the *Eight Stages of Man* and coined the term *identity crisis,* devoted his entire life's work to studying the interplay between culture and identity development. He might say that if you grew up reading tattered books by oil lamp out on the American prairie in the 1800s, the details of your identity would be quite different than if you grew up reading information downloaded from the Internet and displayed on a computer monitor in your perfectly temperature-controlled suburban home. He would also say that, after all is said and done, human beings will always be human beings, and that there are certain universal stages through which we all must pass in order to continue growing.

Thumb Your Nose at Gravity

Charles Lindbergh isn't the only "pearl" to have thumbed his nose at gravity. Martin Seligman is a world-renowned research psychologist who shocked the academic world as a young graduate student in 1965 when he proposed that it was possible for dogs (and, by extrapolation, humans) to learn to be helpless. To understand the enormity of such a proposition, you would have to know that anything that challenged the basic principles of behaviorism was considered heresy back then. The notion of *learned helplessness* went on to become the centerpiece of Seligman's life's work, and eventually evolved into his concept of learned optimism.

He thumbed his nose at gravity, and as with most innovations that turn out to be correct and/or successful, there was a huge risk involved in the position that he took. In his book entitled *Learned Optimism,* he described reactions to him and his research partner, Steven Maier:

> *The behaviorists did not blithely surrender. At our home department in the university, the most venerable professor—he himself had edited the* Journal of Experimental

Psychology for twenty years—wrote me a note saying that a draft of our article made him "physically sick." At an international meeting I was accosted by Skinner's leading disciple—in a men's room of all places—and informed that animals ". . . only learn responses." [7]

Seligman described Steve Maier as "a shy, studious young man from the heart of the Bronx" who had "grown up in poverty . . . and had a taste for struggle." Seligman himself had seen his share of major life struggles, so they persisted in their work. Each time there was a setback in their research findings or an onslaught of professional criticism, they picked themselves up, brushed themselves off and pushed ahead. Charlie Gibson and Diane Sawyer did a special edition of *Good Morning America* one fall day in 1999, and they invited Martin Seligman to be one of the primary expert commentators for the program. In talking about optimism, depression and learned helplessness, Seligman said that *successful people fail, they just never quit.*

In the Greek myth, Daedalus cautions his son, Icarus, not to fly too close to the sun, lest it melt the wax holding the feathers on his man-made wings. Icarus was just a little too impulsive. He flew too close to the sun and plunged to his death. Despite that sad, scary tale, human beings continued trying to fly until one day they did. Being a teenager in any era means taking risks, falling down, brushing yourself off, learning from your mistakes, and then pushing ahead again. No one ever got anywhere in love *or* work without taking risks and making mistakes. The key is to take ever-smarter risks.

We'll always be humans, but we won't always be

watching black-and-white television sets and riding our bicycles to the Saturday matinee, where we pay a quarter for a couple of cartoons, a serial and then a double feature. Times change. Contexts change. Methods of transmitting and sharing information change, but people are pretty much the same. The more we learn from those who preceded us, the more we can create for the future. The Wright brothers made the first manned flight in a winged aircraft. By the time Lindbergh came along, he was already standing on the shoulders of giants.

3

The Cockapoo and the Labrador

It is better to live one day as a lion
than a hundred years as a sheep.

—Italian twenty-lire silver piece, 1930

Once upon a time, there was a twenty-pound cockapoo named Sam, and a yellow Labrador retriever named Abby. Sam and Abby met when they were two years old—fourteen in dog years. They met in the Canadian North Woods under the most extreme conditions. Sam was running with a herd of wild cockapoos that was heading towards the region called Labrador, in search of better hunting grounds. It was the end of autumn, the nights were very cold, and a dusting of fresh snow was on the ground. As the alpha male of the herd, all of the other cockapoos looked up to and admired Sam.

Abby the Labrador had been scouting out new hunting territory herself when she heard the thundering paws of the mighty cockapoo herd as it broke through a clearing in the woods and headed toward Dead Dog's Gorge. The herd suddenly stopped at Sam's command, and he paced back and forth with an intensity that Abby had never seen before. He was contemplating jumping across the gorge. The other cockapoos looked worried. Sam felt they had no choice because the weather was getting so poor, and to go around the gorge would add two days to their journey. He knew it wasn't called Dead Dog's Gorge for nothing—only larger breeds were consistently able to leap across it. For Sam and the other cockapoos, jumping it would be an unparalleled achievement.

Abby thought to herself, "Don't do it, buddy. It would be a crying shame to see such a fine-looking animal take a dive into that gorge." Just as she was saying that, Sam backed up, trotted about twenty yards away from the edge, turned, faced it, and then burst into a full lightning-fast sprint. He was airborne in a flash. He sailed dramatically in an arc and landed front-paws-first on the other side with a solid *whumpfgh!* The other cockapoos burst into thunderous cheers that echoed eerily as if the forest itself was an Olympic stadium. Then Abby looked toward Sam again and noticed that he was favoring both front legs. "Oh, no," she said. "He's hurt."

The other cockapoos looked shocked and afraid. Sam stood tall, faced his herd across the gorge, and said in his most commanding bark, "You will have to go on without me. The survival of the herd is of the utmost importance. It has always been this way and always will be." The others began to weep; some shouted protests. Sam was unwavering. Then Abby emerged from the forest and stepped softly, but confidently, into their midst. She announced, "I jump this gorge every autumn, sometimes with fresh kill in my mouth. First, I will take each of you across the gorge. Then I will nurse Sam back to health. A nobler male I have yet to see in my two years." The silence was stunning as every head whipped around and faced Sam, who with the most regal countenance thought for a moment, then humbly and powerfully said, "Make it so."

Sam stood by and proudly watched Abby carry each member of his herd one by one across the gorge. Tears welled up in his eyes. He held his head high as Abby sailed gracefully through the air, her muscles glistening in the low, late-afternoon sun. Each time, she landed confidently on the other side with a grunt and a thud. His head and heart were in a whirl of ambivalence. It was crucial that he allow himself the luxury of his tears and his regret, as well as his relief and hopes for the safety of his herd. In the same instant, he found himself entranced by the vision of this powerful, graceful female of a different breed. Only her unbelievable athletic prowess and generous heart surpassed her physical beauty. "A more compassionate female I have yet to see in my two years," Sam said to himself.

Sam and the others said their good-byes. On the journey to Labrador, a new alpha male would emerge from the herd. Sam knew that it would take care of itself. Then the haunting words of his father suddenly entered his consciousness. His father had told him that the only way to enter into the full depth of adulthood was to experience a nearly heart-breaking disappointment, deal with it graciously and move on. He had said that every cockapoo was capable of entering this level of existence, but that it was a choice to do so. He had said that every creature on earth is presented with at least one major disappointment in life, and that the choice was therefore not in whether one can avoid disappointment or not, but in how one chooses to handle it when it arrives. Now, Sam knew what his father had meant, and he was deeply grateful for his father's counsel, but he was sad.

"Abby," Sam began, with a calmness he didn't know existed inside of him, "I am quite accustomed to being a leader, solving problems quickly, knowing how to assure others, knowing just what to do. I must admit, I am momentarily stunned."

"Sam, I saw something indescribably distinguished in you the very second I spotted you. My heart actually fluttered for a moment," Abby started. She would have blushed, were Labrador retrievers wont to blush. "From what I have witnessed of you and your herd, the choices you made are consistent with what I thought I was first seeing."

"They weren't easy choices, Abby."

"I was in agony, myself, as I watched the drama unfold. I see no other way it could have worked out, either. All of you were likely to be doomed had you not been able to get across that gorge."

"Yes. Despite the current length of our winter manes, cockapoo fur does not have the insulating properties of Labrador fur. Had you not come along, we all very well could have perished."

"My coming along at just the 'right' time is one of those unexplainable and uncontrollable mysteries of creation. Coincidence. Fate. Luck. Grand Design. It's hard to say for certain. Nonetheless, each of us must choose how to respond to those twists of fate. You could have stubbornly rejected my offer of help, getting caught in your own ego, and ultimately proving that you were not the leader that your herd thought you were."

"I considered all of the possibilities."

"As only one of your depth and wisdom would. And you could have chosen to go with them after I carried all of them across the gorge."

"I thought of that, yes. But their loyalty to me would have slowed them down, again endangering the entire herd."

"Right again, Sam."

"Thank you for your kind compliments, Miss Abby. They soothe the sting of this nearly unbearable loss." (He couldn't believe he had just referred to her as Miss Abby. It was way too familiar. At least among cockapoos.) Then Sam said, with a flutter in his heart equal to hers, "I am in awe of your power and gentility, of your agility and strength, of your compassion; and of how stunning, how beautiful you are." (Again, words flowed from his lips that he could scarcely believe.)

"Sam, thank you," she said, simply.

As happens to everyone now and then, whether they want it to or not, their lives began to turn in a new and unexpected direction, and not without harrowing new challenges. They were somewhere in the Far North wilderness. Sam's front legs were injured. Abby had a heartbreaking decision of her own to make. She knew that the chances of Sam's survival would lessen with each day that they spent in the wilderness, whereas if she were to carry him into civilization, she would be clever enough to get him the medical attention he so desperately needed. She also knew that two dogs as exceptional as them would most likely become domesticated. She had heard of this human practice, and although it would always be possible to return to the wilderness, she also knew that the draw of canine loyalty was difficult once it came into play. If someone cruel befriended them, it would be easy to leave, but if a kind person befriended them, it would be very difficult.

She gently picked up Sam in her mouth, being careful not to hurt him with her powerful jaws, but making sure that she had a strong enough hold so she wouldn't drop him. Maintaining the balance between these two took more energy and concentration than she had ever mustered before. It was getting colder, and Sam was getting weaker. After three days of what amounted to a forced march, Sam finally asked Abby, "Where are we going?"

"To a hospital. If we don't, you'll die."

Sam knew. He understood exactly what Abby was doing, and what a sacrifice it was for her. He knew she didn't need to feel guilty on top of it all, so he said, "We'll get through this. I can feel it in my bones." Abby felt warmer and stronger than ever as they curled up together for the night in another animal's abandoned lair. They were two hours from civilization and their new lives together. As they dozed on and off the rest of the night, they both knew that their chance encounter in the woods would turn out to be a transforming experience. Despite the pain, hunger and cold, they were as grateful as two heroic dogs could ever be.

Part II

The Seven Best Things

4

Become Competent:
You Can't Get Self-Esteem
from Talking to Yourself in Front
of the Mirror or Being Smothered
with Praise

A chief event of life is the day in which we have
encountered a mind that startled us.

—Ralph Waldo Emerson, *Character*, 1844

The Freedom Writers
of Wilson High in Long Beach

In the fall of 1994, brand new, preppy, twenty-three-year-old teacher Erin Gruwell walked into a tough Long Beach high school classroom wondering "What my students will think about me? Will they think I'm out of touch or too preppy? Or worse yet, that I'm too young to be taken seriously?" The class was filled with kids who were leading tragic lives littered with divorce, physical and sexual abuse, drive-by shootings, gangs and drugs. With these as permanent fixtures in their daily lives, what teacher, let alone what new teacher, could expect to have any impact on the kids?

We make a point to always refer to Erin Gruwell and her students when we are teaching the graduate classes that we offer to schoolteachers in the Minneapolis/St. Paul area. We do so because it is one of the most inspirational stories of across-the-board success with a supposedly "doomed" group of teenagers that we have ever encountered. We have yet to watch Connie Chung's *ABC News Primetime Live* report on Erin Gruwell's student group the "Freedom Writers" without being brought to tears.

It all began with the following things. One, there was a classroom filled with ordinary kids, many of whom were from the toughest parts of Long Beach, which means that most of them were indeed, doomed. Second, there was a teacher who had an excellent education herself, so that she actually had something to teach them. Third, there was a classroom filled with ordinary *teenagers,* period. In other words, ordinary teenagers, no matter what their circumstances, want to be competent. The instant that anyone assumes that this is true, the chances of them becoming competent increase logarithmically. Erin Gruwell assumed that they were competent. Last, all of the people in that room were passionate about what they were doing there, even from the beginning. Passion provides the energy that drives the machine. The rest, as they say, is history.

Miss Gruwell, as her students affectionately call her, actually began the year before as a student teacher at Wilson High, where she snatched up a racist drawing that one student had made of another. Furious at the intolerance expressed in the picture, she yelled that it reminded her of the Holocaust. When a student timidly asked what the Holocaust was, Erin Gruwell threw away the textbooks and started teaching *to* these kids instead of *at* them. Most of the kids in her class had either been shot, shot at or witnessed gang shootings. They had experienced the other traumas of living in troubled neighborhoods, so they could relate to the Holocaust. They went to see Steven Spielberg's *Schindler's List* in Newport Beach, the gated community where she lived, only to be treated rudely by some of the bigoted people in the theater who were shocked that she would bring her students there. One of her neighbors told her, "If you love black people so much, why don't you just marry a monkey?" The local newspaper ran a front-page story in her defense.

She pressed on and had her students read *Anne Frank: The Diary of a Young Girl.* She brought in a Holocaust survivor.

She had her students read Zlata Filipovic's book *Zlata's Diary: A Child's Life in Sarajevo,* a fifteen-year-old girl's story of living in war-ravaged Sarajevo. The students raised money to fly Filipovic to Southern California to visit them. Then Erin Gruwell's students began writing. She had them write diaries to process their experiences and feelings, and they nicknamed themselves "The Freedom Writers" after the freedom riders of the civil rights movement in the 1960s. When these kids started with Miss Gruwell, they could expect not to live very long. Their lives were dead-ends. They were hopeless. By the time they finished high school, all 150 of them were bound for college. A book of their diary entries was published as *The Freedom Writers Diary: How a Teacher and 150 Teens Used Writing to Change Themselves and the World Around Them.* The authors' proceeds from the book are used to fund the Tolerance Education Foundation, which was set up to help pay for the Freedom Writers' college tuition.

Shame, Shame

We now ask you to shift gears and imagine that you're a second-grader at your local public school. You're having a hard time reading a certain passage from the reader that you and your classmates are working on. It's your turn to read aloud, and you can feel your face flushing and your skin crawling as you sink deeper and deeper into a black hole of embarrassment and paralysis. Your brain locks. You're staring down at the page, but nothing is coming to you. It's all over. You pray that your teacher leaves you alone and moves on to the next student. For some reason—maybe she had a fight with her husband this morning, maybe you remind her of her older brother who tormented her when she was a child—she yells louder and commands you to look up at her. She yells, "Billy Torgerson, you march right up here to the front of the class and put on that dunce cap and sit in the corner for fifteen minutes! You're just not trying!"

The humiliation is overpowering, but you have no options. You begrudgingly comply as the laughter and taunts of your classmates drown out even your own inner talk. You march up there, don the tall pointed hat of shame, the symbol of failure and ignorance, and sit on the stool facing the corner. The titters and giggles continue until she quiets them all down and continues with the reading practice. Your spirit feels as if it has shattered. It is hard to imagine ever feeling worse about yourself. Your only hope is that you'll still be intact when this horrible day finally comes to a close.

And More Shame

In April 1999, Oprah Winfrey had us on her show for an hour to discuss our previous book, *The 7 Worst Things (Good) Parents Do.* As part of the show, Oprah's staff had found a very kind and courageous mother and daughter who were willing to demonstrate the first "worst thing" from our book, which is to baby our children. The daughter was a single young woman in her early twenties with a little girl of her own. The mother explained that she had a painful childhood herself, and so she wanted to make her own daughter's childhood painless by doing everything for her and just letting her be. As you probably guessed, the daughter explained that her mother's good intentions had prevented the daughter from growing up. The daughter never learned how to take care of herself, how to *enjoy* struggle, how to handle her emotions, how to keep herself safe or how to eventually live on her own.

It was a powerful experience to see these two loving women struggle so gallantly with such a difficult predicament. The mother very candidly said that she *still* had a hard time stopping herself from doing things for her daughter that she knew her daughter should do for herself. She shared that she would even go over to her daughter's place and do her laundry for her when she knew her daughter had endured a stressful day. Her daughter acknowledged how seriously depressed she had become when starting college because being out on her own was completely overwhelming—she simply was not prepared for life. She got into drinking, partying and having sex without thinking of the consequences because she had never learned that her actions have consequences.

It's Alive!

We have been talking about the flaws in the self-esteem movement for at least a decade, and the two examples we just outlined above capture the essence of the problem as we see it. The self-esteem movement began a few decades ago in response to the terrible discipline practices that were considered very acceptable at the time. It was accepted and culturally approved to belittle and humiliate children "to teach them a lesson," and it was always done "for your own good." In fact, Alice Miller's groundbreaking book on child abuse had the same title: *For Your Own Good.* To put a dunce cap on a child's head and then make him sit in front of the classroom to be laughed at by all the other children is unquestionably a cruel, hostile act, and any social movement designed to stop such practices is to be applauded.

The problem is in what happened next. As the self-esteem movement began to grow, psychologists and educators won more and more grants, did more and more research, and wrote more and more articles on self-esteem. *Then* something right out of the *X-Files* happened. What began as a useful hypothetical construct suddenly took on a life of its own, becoming a living entity inside of each little child. "It's alive!" That's what scientist Victor Frankenstein exclaimed in director James Whale's 1931 version of the film *Frankenstein,* made famous by Boris Karloff's stunning performance as "the monster." That's what parents, teachers and researchers all over the United States exclaimed, too, when speaking about self-esteem: "It's alive!"

The trouble with the whole concept is that self-esteem isn't an entity inside of us, and it certainly doesn't *cause* anything. In fact, self-esteem is *itself* caused by something else. It is simply a summary variable, a descriptor that helps scientists talk to each other in shorthand. To say that little Bobby is doing poorly in school because he has low self-esteem is like saying that little Bobby's Grandpa can't remember where he left his false teeth because he's ninety-two years old! It's nonsense. Grandpa can't remember where he left his false teeth because he has lost a certain number of brain cells, or because the blood circulation to his brain has been restricted due to arteriosclerosis, or because he has Alzheimer's disease. Not all ninety-two-year-olds have memory problems, and age itself doesn't cause anything, as geropsychologists Warner Schaie, Paul Baltes and John Nesselroade sagely noted nearly thirty years ago.

The truth is that little Bobby may be doing poorly in school because no one at home is encouraging him to learn anything, or because nobody is at home, period. He may be doing poorly because he has a mistaken belief that he isn't capable of learning. It may be because no one at home knows how to learn things and so he has no one to watch to see how to learn things. He may have a learning disability. He may not be sleeping enough at night due to his parents' constant fighting. He may not be eating enough. He may have some kind of chronic illness. He may have paralyzing anxiety because his parents constantly scream at him and criticize him at home.

Do you see the difference? If we say that little Bobby has trouble learning because he has low self-esteem, then we might think that we could solve his learning problem by *raising his self-esteem.* How have experts typically tried to do that? They praise kids too much and teach them to tell themselves that they're wonderful. As Dr. Sylvia Rimm points out in her book, *Dr. Sylvia Rimm's Smart Parenting,* "Children who become attention addicted at home are likely to feel, by comparison, attention deprived at school."[8] What happens if kids don't know anything, but are continually encouraged to see themselves as the greatest? The result is narcissism, grandiosity, incompetence and eventually failure. None of these qualities does much for a kid's self-esteem.

If we say he has trouble learning because he *doesn't know how to learn,* then our strategy will be to teach him *how to learn.* What a novel concept! He may be having trouble learning because no one at home is encouraging him to learn. If this is the case, we could either encourage the people at home to value learning or we could make sure that we make the classroom really interesting for little Bobby and make it worth his while to learn. Maybe we could even ask for help from people like the history teacher in the previous chapter.

Competence and Real Intimacy: The Cures for the Self-Esteem Dilemma

Here's the secret formula: For anyone who feels that she suffers from low self-esteem, there are only two things that will make a difference, and they will both make all the difference in the world.

Competence

First, we have to become *competent.* Work addicted? No. CEO of a Fortune 500 company? No. President of the school board? No. Mayor? No, just competent. Every human being has the potential to become competent for her age and intellectual strengths and limits. We know a man who is twenty-six years old and has Down's syndrome. He has an IQ of about fifty-five. He is one of the most competent people we know. Is he limited in ways that you aren't? Probably.

As the authors of this book, we are both successful therapists, but neither of us will ever become astrophysicists because neither of us has the kind of intelligence needed for such an accomplishment. John likes to read popular articles about the universe, but he acknowledges that his intelligence and academic training limit his understanding of those articles.

Over the years of our private practice in psychology, we have worked with doctors, lawyers, plumbers, geneticists, psychiatrists, electricians, investment bankers, teachers, laborers, accountants, retail clerks, psychologists, housewives, real estate agents, bank tellers, students, construction workers, stay-at-home-dads, you name it. No matter who it is or what they do for a living, we find ourselves saying silently, *"This person knows so much more than I do about. . . ."* People who think that we just sit in our offices day after day and listen to problems don't get it. If that's what a psychologist in private practice does every day, he should retire, and do so immediately. People come to us for *our* expertise, but they each have *their own expertise* for which we honor them and hold them in the highest esteem.

We hold them in the highest esteem because each of them is competent at something. If they aren't competent at something yet, they have taken the life-changing risk to admit it and start the process of becoming competent, and thereby demonstrate their competence by the very fact of admitting their limitations! Self-esteem is about stretching beyond one's *perceived* limitations. The man with Down's syndrome stretched by testifying in front of his state senate about what it's like to be intellectually challenged. A gifted neurosurgeon with whom we worked stretched by sitting in a room with his wife and children as he wept about how lonely he felt as a little boy. An incredibly brilliant and successful craftsman we knew stretched far beyond his own perceived limitations by talking about the dyslexia that he had kept secret for seventy-two years.

The National Education Commission on Time and Learning reported in 1994 that kids in this country spend about 41 percent of their school day on academics, leaving 59 percent for something else. Over the four years of high school in the United States, the typical student spends about 1,460 hours on subjects like math, science and history. In Japan, that same figure is 3,170 hours. In France, it's 3,280. In Germany, it's 3,528. In a 1993 report by the United States Department of Education, the vast majority of Americans said that they could read and write "well" or "very well," although in actuality 47 percent of those Americans had a low level of literacy.

In a 1992 Louis Harris survey of high school graduates who had been out of school for from four to eight years, 68 percent said they had learned math well, and 65 percent of their parents rated their child's high school as teaching math well. When employers were asked if recent high school graduates had sufficient math skills, only 22 percent said "yes." When it came to reading ability, 78 percent of the students said they had been taught well, 67 percent of the parents agreed, and only 30 percent of the employers concurred. With writing, it was even worse, with 66 percent of the students and 56 percent of the parents believing that the students were well prepared, while only *12 percent* of the employers agreed! If you think it's just the business world that views young people as ill prepared, note that staff at colleges and universities reported that among recent high school graduates, only 27 percent were proficient in math, 33 percent in reading, and 18 percent in writing.[9]

American schoolchildren usually rank themselves number one in math and science worldwide. The harsh reality, however, is that when they are compared with children in other countries, our kids often rank somewhere around twelfth to fifteenth. This disturbing fact only serves to reinforce what we have been saying about the damaging effects of the self-esteem movement in its extreme form. When it's twenty degrees below zero outside and your furnace is broken, which repairperson will you want: the one who feels good about himself but doesn't really know much about furnaces or the one who can fix your furnace faster than you can say "Popsicle"?

Suppose that you're the furnace repairperson who feels good about himself, but who can't repair furnaces very well. You go from one house call to the next, but each time you strike out, and the homeowner has to call another person to get the job done. You *feel bad* about failing, so before you go to the next call, you look in the mirror, sort of like Al

Franken's Stuart Smalley character on *Saturday Night Live,* and you say to yourself, "I'm good enough, I'm smart enough, and doggone it, people like me!" How many times can you fail and then try to pump yourself up and then fail again, before you finally feel so bad about yourself that you just want to crawl under a rock and die? Wouldn't it make a lot more sense and be a lot more effective if you just went back and took some refresher courses on furnace repair or you developed an apprentice relationship with a master furnace repairperson? Wouldn't your self-esteem be a lot better if, when you went out to repair furnaces, you could actually repair furnaces? Of course it would. There's no doubt about it. Being competent at something is one of the two keys to having true self-esteem.

Acceptance and Belonging

The second key to cure low self-esteem is to start hanging around people who can accept you for who you are instead of for who they think you should be. This does not mean, by the way, that the people you start hanging around with have to praise you constantly and indiscriminately. If they did, they'd be guilty of the same error that emerged from the self-esteem movement. Acceptance and belonging are different than that. In a healthy family, everybody fits in no matter how different they might be. The tall ones, the short ones, the males, the females, the old ones, the young ones, the ones who are good at math, the ones who can't add fractions, the artistic ones, the loud ones, the introverts— they all fit in and belong.

Unlike people with an inflated sense of themselves, people with high self-esteem have a very accurate perception of themselves, including their limitations. Here is what such a person would say. "I am really proud of this drawing that I just finished for my art class. It's the best thing I've done all year. I'm so glad that my teacher encouraged me to pursue this talent of mine." A little later you might hear the same person say, "You know, I am so bad at math that it's embarrassing sometimes. I was in the hardware store the other day, trying to figure out how much paint to buy for my bedroom, and the clerk must have thought I just fell off of a turnip truck or something, I was having such a difficult time." In describing his childhood, this same person might explain that, "My parents have been very understanding as I've grown up. My math difficulties showed up pretty early, they had me tested, I got some tutoring, and I struggled my way through it. They never said that I didn't have to learn math because they knew I needed to learn it. We'd have a lot of battles about it as I grew up, but they never said that I was stupid, and I always felt like I was okay—you know— an equal member of the family. They didn't need me to be great at math any more than they needed my sister to be great at art. They just wanted to make sure that each of us had the basic skills we needed to get along in the world."

A sense of belonging is one of the most important and powerful forces in any human being's life, yet it is conveyed in such a quiet, simple way in most cases. Sure, there are those dramatic moments, like when you win the art contest or get a scholarship to study math in college. In these cases, family members hoot and holler and celebrate, but those events don't happen very often. A sense of belonging is a pretty constant experience in a healthy family. It is conveyed in a lot of ordinary, matter-of-fact ways that, when combined, add up to the foundation for everything else in our lives.

This is why we have said repeatedly over the years that the little things in life, the ordinary everyday things, are usually the most important. A good film director knows that. He'll focus on a look, a glance, a pat on the back, an upturned brow, or a tiny gesture of kindness. Dad walks through the kitchen on his way to the garage, and passes by his son, who is standing at the kitchen counter reading the front page of the morning newspaper. *Almost* as an afterthought, Dad brushes by his son, pats him on the shoulder quickly, asks "How ya' doin'?" and then continues on into the garage. Imagine the limitless possibilities in this little scenario. Imagine how many different messages this father could convey to his son simply by changing one little feature in this brief interaction. What if he had a barely perceptible edge of sarcasm or irritation in his voice, as if to say "How ya' doin'? And by the way, while you're standing there enjoying yourself, you lazy good-for-nothing kid, why don't you think about mowing the lawn like you said you'd do three days ago?"

After being around the same people for awhile, we know whether or not it's safe to let down our guard. That's another way to measure whether you feel like you belong or not. If the people in your family are critical, nitpicky types, then after awhile you'll know deep down inside that it just isn't safe in the same way it's safe at your best friend's house, for example. At first, it's hard to pin down what's going on in a family like this, too, but if you get good at what we call "noticing and listening," you'll be able to discern what the pattern is. Mom asks, "Are you going to wear *that* to the party?" "Yes," you reply, "jeans and a sport shirt with a button-down collar are what most of the guys wear to parties these days." Your Dad asks why you think you want to major in chemistry when you get to college, but it isn't an innocent curiosity that underlies his question. You can tell from the tone in his voice that he's disappointed in your choice of chemistry. You don't know why. You don't know why it should matter to him. It's your life. *Why can't they just accept me for who I am every once in awhile?* you ask yourself.

When a family comes in to do some therapy work, one of the things we often try to do is to help them see these "invisible" patterns that exist in all families. Invariably, as Dad and Mom begin to see the level of negativity and criticism that they have created, they will say that they never intended it to have that effect. They'll say that they were just trying to be concerned, loving parents. They were just trying to be helpful. Their parents were that way, and they didn't mean any harm by it. If they stay with it and struggle until they let their defenses down a little more, they can eventually admit that they let their *anxiety* take control of them, and that no excuses justify their children walking on eggshells all the time. They will eventually be able to say that they are sorry.

One of the most important things that happens after a person has been in one of our therapy groups for about nine months is that this deeper sense of belonging begins to appear. You might think that nine months is a long time, but when you realize what a pervasive phenomenon we're dealing with, and how deep into our souls it goes, nine months isn't long at all. Even though we've seen it appear in hundreds and hundreds of people over the years, when this sense of acceptance and belonging begins to appear it feels like a miracle is happening right before our very eyes. Remember that there are no bells and whistles, no fireworks, no sirens, no orchestras or choirs accompanying this event. It appears in a look, a glance, a new level of comfort, a willingness to experience feelings more openly, or in giving more appropriate feedback to other group members. It shows up in small, ordinary, everyday ways, and when it does, the person begins to heal with a depth he or she never knew was possible.

Some of the "Competency Traps" That May Plague Teenagers

There are numerous things that can get in your way on the road to becoming a competent person. Below, we discuss a few of them.

Becoming Competent Isn't Cool

In chapter 5, we quote a teenager who was kind enough to share some of her high school struggles. One of them was the inner battle she experienced between the strong desire to fit in with her peers and the desire to do well in school.

In *Reviving Ophelia,* psychologist Mary Pipher noted that, "Junior high is when girls begin to fade academically." She then quoted a couple of girls who told her, "Either way I lose. If I make a good grade, they are mad. If I make a bad grade, they spread it around that even I can screw up," and "I figured out that I'd have more friends if I focused on sports. Smart girls were nerds."[10]

The reference group that we compare ourselves to is very important, no matter what our age, but it is especially important during the teen years. If kids can occasionally take a glimpse past high school and look at life from the point of view of a young adult, they can sometimes make the leap across the gorge that separates academic success and academic failure. Of course, it is much easier for a teenager to get that glimpse into the future if her mother and father value her achievement and encourage it by their own achievements, and they take an interest in what she is learning. It is very important to remember that things can turn around—there is always hope. Mary Pipher quoted a girl who said, "My friends and I decided that making good grades wasn't cool," but noted that the following year, in eighth grade, the girl and her friends decided that it was now cool to get good grades, which they then did.[11]

Don't Ever Assume That You Can't Become Competent

Books, newspapers, magazines, films and television news programs are filled with inspirational stories about kids who overcame insurmountable odds and went on to an adulthood of remarkable accomplishments. We have always found that learning about the lives of others who overcame those odds helps us in our own personal struggles. In our practice, we see many people who look at another person's inspirational life and exclaim, "But I'm not that kind of person! I'm just ordinary." To which we matter-of-factly respond, "Everyone is ordinary. That's what being a human being is about."

Beware of Things That Suck the Life Out of You

Sometimes it is hard to decide which is worse: to suck the life and will out of a child by cruel treatment, or to suck the life and will out of a child by spoiling and indulging him. Psychologically, it makes little sense to compare types of child maltreatment. We can affirm that when children grow up amidst wealth and privilege with parents who make few efforts to make sure their kids have to struggle, the end result is not a pretty sight. Few things suck the life out of a human being faster than letting him believe that he can have everything, all the time, and with no struggle. *Struggle is good.*

In an article written for the *Wall Street Journal,* Nancy Ann Jeffrey focused on the painful struggles that have emerged in the families that have benefited from the newly acquired wealth of the 1990s. Parents are increasingly worried that if they don't pay attention, they will produce a generation of spoiled, narcissistic, overly entitled children who have no drive and no values. Ms. Jeffrey referred to this potential brat backlash as "bratlash," an apt description for what we see going on in some families.[12] If you are in the middle of this kind of trap, you may not even be aware of it. If you are aware of it, you may feel so seduced by the largesse that you can't say "no" to it. After all, if your parents can't say "no" to it at all, who could expect you to? In situations like this, one of the best things you can do is to let yourself remain aware that when you get a little older, one of your most important tasks may be to find some "soul-building" experiences—struggles that will help to pull you back into life.

By the way, on the "up" side of the story, Ms. Jeffrey cited a survey done by a financial planning firm in which they looked at allowances given to children in households with incomes between $100,000 and $900,000. "More than 40 percent gave their children allowances of between two and ten dollars a week. Many parents required children to do chores to get their allowance, and some required that children earmark portions for savings and charity. A few parents gave weekly allowances of between twenty and thirty dollars. The richest parents didn't give bigger allowances than ones who made less."[13]

So Now You Have It

Here is a final lesson in competence that we learned long ago. When we were in elementary school, our teachers told us to keep a dictionary right next to us whenever we were reading a book, newspaper, magazine or school assignment. They said that it would help us know what the words meant when it came time to be tested on what we'd read. They also said that this would be the best way to insure that we would become successful in our careers later in life. We weren't completely convinced at the time, but we did as we were told. Now that we are published authors, we know that they were right.

5

Master Your Feelings:
Don't Let the Tail Wag the Dog

No one is free who commands not himself.

—Epictetus, *Encheridion,* c. 110 A.D.

The emotional part of your brain is overheating. Well, not exactly. That was an overreaction. Pardon the pun, but it does react differently than it will in a few years. Neuropsychologists have discovered that because of the developmental changes going on in teenagers' bodies, their emotional reactions tend to be more intense than they were before or after adolescence. Having been teenagers ourselves once, we find it very comforting to read this data. There is enough for you to do between thirteen and twenty without being completely misunderstood or misinterpreted by the adults around you.

When it comes to excellence in scientific writing about feelings, Daniel Goleman is at the top of our list. A psychologist as well as a journalist for the *New York Times,* Goleman wrote a brilliant bestselling book a few years ago that focused on a group of skills that many contemporary people seem to be lacking, and he organized them under the heading of *Emotional Intelligence.* We were especially excited about the book because as practicing psychologists we find ourselves helping many people (1) *identify* their feelings as part of their therapy work with us. Some people also ask our help in learning to (2) *express* their feelings more clearly and accurately. We also work with some people to help them (3) *contain* their emotions because their emotions often get the best of them.

How It Works: Making Conscious the Unconscious Rules of Living

The ability to identify, express and contain our emotions is supposed to be learned in our families as we are growing up. Growing up in a family system from birth to twenty-one has been likened to a hypnotic process in which we are embedded in the family, and as we go about our daily lives we simply *absorb* all of the unconscious rules of living that are around us. Some people actually believe that the experience of their feelings "has always been that way." They also believe that it is not possible to reeducate themselves about the way they experience their feelings, but we have worked with thousands of people who have learned otherwise. You *can* contain your feelings so that they don't spill over and hurt you or others.

First, let's look at how the rules in a family are learned. As you read the next couple of sentences, see if you can spot where a couple of volatile feelings might set up the possibility of a family explosion if they aren't handled well. Suppose that you're watching television or reading a book, and you notice out of the corner of your eye that Mom can't find her car keys. She walks into the kitchen where your Dad is fixing himself a sandwich and says, "I meant to thank you for taking my car this afternoon and filling my gas tank. I really appreciate it when you do that. By the way, do you remember where you put my keys? I need to run a quick errand." See? You were just exposed to some very powerful unconscious rules about how to relate to another person, especially a loved one. You would learn very different rules if Mom walked into the kitchen and said, "Where the hell are my car keys? I am *so* sick and tired of having to look for my keys every time you take my car. You think you're doing me a favor, but . . . get a grip! You're not! I can fill my *own* gas tank, for crying out loud!"

Being a member of a family system is an incredible experience from a purely scientific standpoint. Regardless of how supportive or how painful one's family is, how a family functions is one of the most interesting things we can think of studying. So let's look at another example of how these unconscious rules of living get transmitted to everyone in the system.

Imagine for a moment that you are an eighteen-month-old sitting in your highchair just quietly chewing on a cracker and thoughtfully observing everything that's going on around you. As you put yourself in that little child's position, you might even want to put this book down for a moment, close your eyes, and visualize what's going on around you as you chew on that cracker. Dad is in the living room reading a book. Mom is sitting at the table near you, working the *New York Times* crossword puzzle. Your five-year-old sister is sitting on the floor in the living room, on the edge of the kitchen between you and Dad. She is quietly talking herself through an attempt to stack some blocks higher than she did yesterday. In the background, you can hear the national news coming from the radio.

Okay. Open your eyes for a moment and notice what you're thinking. Now notice what you're feeling. For some of you, this may be a familiar scene, while for others it may be so foreign that it's difficult to imagine at all. If you are good at visualizing, or if you practice until you become better at it, what you'll notice is that you'll be able to identify all sorts of details in that simple scenario that we just described for you. Some people begin to notice that they are really taking on the perspective of that eighteen-month-old in the highchair. They begin to see through the little child's eyes. It is as if a 360-degree camera is feeding images back to them through their computers.

When you get good at this sort of visualizing, you may begin to notice many other details in this scene. You may notice that Mom screws up her face in a certain way when she encounters an especially difficult spot in the crossword puzzle. You may notice that when your older sister's tower of blocks comes crashing down, she immediately stops and

gets calm, just for a split-second, and then she says something like, "Darn! They crashed!" Then you notice her face
take on a very pensive gaze, and you hear her say, "I need to
build a wider base before I try to make it that high!" Then
you see your father's head pop up from the newspaper, and
he looks at what she's doing and responds to what she just
said, "You're doing a good job of figuring that out." You
notice a different look on his face—he seems pleased and
interested. Then you remember that when you and he were
playing on the floor with the blocks the other day, he did
the same thing—he talked out loud as he stacked the blocks
one on the other. He said out loud what he was thinking in
his head.

Do you see the exquisite subtlety with which the rules in
a family are transmitted to each person? At this point you
might be thinking, "That was a pretty far-fetched example.
What American household operates like *that?*" You'd be
partially correct. Not all American households operate like
that. You might be surprised to learn that many do, though.
Even if this kind of household is a rarity, it's a lot easier to
demonstrate what we're talking about than if we began by
using a household that lives in chaos. The important thing
to learn here is that what we just took you through is what
thousands of people examine when they come in for therapy
in attempts to salvage their relationships and their families.
It's exactly like the process you go through when you try to
fix your car's engine or when you try to keep your new
browser software from crashing every time it loads a certain
plug-in. You can't fix what you haven't admitted is broken,
and you can't fix it if you don't know how it works.

We should mention that psychologist John Gottman at the University of Washington has been studying the non-verbal communications between couples for over twenty-five years, and has identified hundreds of different subtleties in tone of voice, facial expression, gesture and posture that each sends a powerful message to the other person. He has gotten so good at this that he can now predict with 94-percent accuracy whether a couple's marriage will last or not, just by looking at these subtle messages that we each send to other people all day long. It's truly remarkable, and exciting.

Nothing More Than Feelings, and Nothing Less, Either

Feelings "Just Happen"

The study of human feelings is one of the most fascinating pursuits a psychologist can follow. As Daniel Goleman described so elegantly in *Emotional Intelligence,* feelings are neurochemical reactions that occur in the limbic system of the brain. This is sometimes called the "reptilian brain" because feelings "just happen"—we don't have a lot of control over *whether they occur or not.* A reptile simply reacts without thinking of the consequences. A rattlesnake doesn't think to himself, "This man who almost stepped on me is Abraham Lincoln. If I bite him, he may die, changing the whole course of human history. I'd better not bite him!" The snake just reacts. It is the consummate *reactor.*

In human beings, feelings "just happen" also. Suppose a very competent surgeon comes to us because she is about to lose her job. The hospital where she practices has sent a personnel file indicating that she has been blowing up at everyone at work, causing mayhem regularly. When we ask her what she feels as she is describing these embarrassing and painful circumstances to us, she might say, "I don't feel anything right now. They have their point of view, and I have mine. I haven't done anything wrong. I'm thinking of suing them." We know that it is physiologically impossible for her to not feel anything right now because the reptilian brain in each of us "just reacts." What we *suspect* is that she is feeling a lot of shame (embarrassment), perhaps some fear (of what will happen to her), maybe some loneliness (because she has been cut off from her colleagues), and then, to cover it all up and protect herself (which is a perfectly sensible thing to do), we suspect she's feeling angry. Are we being presumptuous here? Arrogant? Are we mind readers? No. It's just a simple fact of humanity that under these circumstances, we'll feel those feelings.

If you really want to get a handle on what we just wrote, pay close attention to your own reactions when something happens to you *abruptly* and *without warning.* For example, you're driving (or riding) down the freeway at sixty miles per hour, and out of nowhere a car cuts in front of you aggressively and wildly. You're startled. What does "startled" mean? It means anxious, nervous, scared, afraid, frightened— you pick the word, they're all the same feeling. What do many people say they feel in this situation? They say "mad, angry, pissed, annoyed, ticked off"—they all mean the same. Who's right? Here's what's true: If you pay attention to what's going on inside your body, you'll notice that when someone cuts you off on the freeway like that, your heart rate increases, your blood pressure goes up, and your breathing gets rapid and shallow for a second. Those are startle reactions. Startle reactions are just another way of saying "fear."

When we try to explain this to people who need to deny that they feel fear, they get angry with us for suggesting that they might feel fear. They might have been so hurt when they were children that the only way they could make it through childhood was to ignore the fear. Or they might have been belittled and criticized after telling adults when they felt scared, which would make them feel very frightened and embarrassed to say that they ever feel fear. Just because I *believe* that I'm not afraid doesn't mean that I don't *feel* afraid. Remember: Feelings happen in the reptilian brain, in the limbic system. Feelings "just happen."

And Then More Advanced Creatures Think About Feelings, Except When Acting Like Snakes

Back to our example. You get startled on the freeway, feel the fright, then quickly burn inside. You're suddenly enraged. Now what? As an advanced creature who has both a reptilian brain and a mammalian brain with a very well-developed cerebral cortex, you get more options. If you're emotionally intelligent, you'll notice that you were startled, anxious, scared. Then you'll notice that as a protective reaction you begin to get really mad. Then you *think:* "I'd like to run that SOB off the road. Who the hell does he think he is?" Then you *think ahead:* "But if I overreact here, I might really try to run him off the road, and that would have disastrous consequences for him, me and God knows who else." *Then you decide:* "Take a deep breath. Relax. Shake off the anxiety. Good. Now get out of the fast lane. Move over into the middle lane. Let the fool go, and hope he doesn't kill himself or somebody else."

Having a cerebral cortex changes many of the rules of living and gives each of us the joint burdens/advantages of empathy and social responsibility. The snake gets scared and simply goes ahead and bites, out of self-defense. *We* get scared, and then we have a whole range of consequences and decisions to sift through, if we so choose. If we choose not to use our cerebral cortex, then all we have to do is "bite" and ask questions later. This works in a few limited emergency situations. In all others, it typically leads to tragedy, as in the way-too-common domestic homicide case below:

Husband asks, "You had an affair with whom?" Having little emotional intelligence, husband is unaware of the fear and shame and hurt that he feels upon hearing of his wife's infidelity, and instead escalates directly into rage. He reaches for gun and shoots wife. Bullet severs aorta. Wife dies instantly. Subject bursts into tears after realizing what a terrible, irreversible act he has committed. Seven-year-old daughter, now suffering from shock, watched entire scene from corner of kitchen after being awakened by loud fighting of parents. Thinking it was just another marital fight, neighbors had waited to call police. Police arrived on scene two minutes too late to stop the shooting.

It would be scientifically correct if the headlines read: Baby-Man Who Chose Not to Think Used Puny Brain of Snake to Kill Wife While Seven-Year-Old Daughter Watched. What a perfectly preventable tragedy.

Feelings Happen in Our Bodies

Yes, feelings are registered in the brain, but they are felt in the body. If you are having trouble identifying what you're feeling, don't try to "figure it out." Simply let your eyes glance downward, take a deep breath, even close your eyes if possible, and notice what your body is doing. Are your hands cold and clammy? Is your heart racing? Is your breathing shallow? Is your stomach doing butterflies? That's usually fear. Are your muscles tense and ready to fight? Are you grinding your teeth? Is there "fire in your belly"? That's probably anger. Do you feel dirty, broken, disgusted deep down in the pit of your stomach? That's often shame.

80 Percent of the Expression of Feelings Is Nonverbal

The words you say are almost irrelevant when you are try-ing to connect *emotionally* with another person. Notice what message will be conveyed to me if you stare at me blankly and, with a monotone voice and no facial expressions or changes in body posture, you say, "I am so excited that you stopped by to visit. You are my best friend. I am so happy." Your words will say one thing and your nonverbals another. This is called "crazy-making" for obvious reasons. The message will be *so* confusing. In families where expressing emotions is not done well, or not done much at all, everything else can be going very smoothly, but children growing up in such families will have a fair bit of damage to repair, as adults, if they ever want a good intimate relationship with another.

Feelings Are Going on All the Time

Feelings "just happen," *and* they're going on all the time. When we do one of our 3½-day ClearLife Therapy Clinics, we give a lecture on feelings early in the process. At some point in the lecture, we'll mention that feelings are happening all the time, and then we'll suggest that each participant has probably felt most of the primary feelings already that day, if only for an instant. We then ask people if they can recall feeling some of those feelings since getting up in the morning. Anger? "Somebody was driving so slow in front of me." Sad and scared? "I spoke with my wife back home and she said that a friend of ours was just diagnosed with cancer." Happy? "I was really glad to get here this morning and talk with the people in my group." Ashamed? "When you mentioned the craziness of saying one thing but not having the nonverbals to match it, I do that, I'm embarrassed to say."

If feelings are going on all the time, then it makes this whole business of mastering one's emotions much easier. You don't have to wonder if they're there, you just have to find them. If you believe that you are feeling nothing some-times (as in, "I'm dead or in a coma"), then it would be pretty hard to master your emotions. If we are *dissociated,* i.e., disconnected, from our feelings a lot, then we'll be feeling things, but not be aware of it. When that happens, we become *slaves* to our emotions. For example, if your parents have a scary fight ending with your dad storming out of the house with threats of divorce, your mom will feel fear, hurt, sadness, shame, anger, loneliness and maybe even flashes of relief that at least the fight is over for now. If she doesn't allow herself to be conscious of those feelings, they may get the best of her. You might walk in and ask her if you can go to a friend's house for the night. She might *rage* at you instead of thinking it through and realizing that she's unconsciously *afraid* you might be leaving, too. In other words, when we dissociate from our feelings, we do a lot of reptilian things.

When we accept that feelings are always there, all we have to do is take a moment to look for them. If you are dis-connected from your feelings a lot already, this will take some effort. It can take a highly intellectualized person a year or more of regular practice to be able to readily iden-tify what she's feeling. Once you learn to do it, your feelings will become incredible allies that help guide you instead of tyrants that prompt you to do terrible things. *Assume they're there, then notice them now and then.*

The Primary Colors of the Emotional World, All of Which Are "Good"

There are numerous lists of basic feelings, and they all vary a little from one to the other. The list we use is one we have used for over twenty years, and it has worked well for our clients and us. As you look over the list, please remember that every single emotion that human beings feel is good. While some feelings are uncomfortable, there are no "bad" feelings. There's a big difference between "bad" and "uncomfortable." Pain is uncomfortable, but without it we would get damaged over and over in the same way and in the same place. Obviously, pain is good. Sadness is uncomfortable, but it is the emotion that lets us heal from loss, and so it is like the immune system of the psychological world. Obviously, sadness is good. So, here is our list of feelings with brief descriptions attached.

Safety/Warmth/Dependency

Even before you are born, you will feel this if your mother's pregnancy is relatively normal. The sense of safety is actually felt as warmth because the blood vessels in the periphery of our arms and legs will relax and open up when we feel safe, increasing the blood flow to our hands and feet. The ability to depend on others is a crucial part of being a successful human being, too. Dependency is only a problem in its extremes—*too dependent or too independent.* A child who is too independent at too early of an age is headed for dependency problems in adulthood, whether it is chemical dependency, some other addiction, or exaggerated relationship dependencies. So is a child who is kept helpless and dependent too long.

As St. Paul psychologist Bill Doherty noted in *Take Back Your Kids,* parents have let their relationship with their kids become one of "provider of services" for their children, the "consumers."[14] Healthy parents who understand the importance of balance will let children lean on them as much as they *need* to, but not necessarily as much as they *want* to. At each stage of our lives, there are challenges that we must face in order to grow up. Wise parents let us struggle with those challenges rather than making everything too easy for us. Wise parents also realize that when we are children, we are children, so they don't expect us to do adult things—like listen to their personal problems—which would be destructive to us.

Anger

Anger is required to set boundaries and to protect us. It also provides the energy to create change. You poke me, I get mad and ask you to stop. You kill my daughter while you're driving drunk, and I get so mad that I change the drunk-driving laws across the entire nation, like Candy Lightner did through her Mothers Against Drunk Driving (MADD). In its extreme forms, it appears as rage, which is uncontrolled anger, or as passive-aggressive anger, which often seems like an almost sickening "niceness." People who try to be perfectly "nice" all the time often complain about how someone else in their life is always raging, but it is a common pattern for an "overt rager" to be paired up with a "covert rager." If the "nice" one decides to grow and starts to express some *healthy* anger, the explosive one often calms way down. In other words, "nicey-nice," as we sometimes call it, isn't really nice at all. It only looks that way.

Anger is always triggered by one of the "softer" emotions—hurt, shame or fear. Because anger is there to protect us and to set boundaries, whenever we feel threatened by something, anger kicks in to protect us. It's easy to see how this works with a physical threat, such as someone hitting you. It also comes into play with a threat to your self, your identity, your personhood. So, if someone "hits" you emotionally by attacking you with words in front of everyone at school, you'll feel some shame, maybe some fear, and maybe your feelings will be hurt. Then you may get angry. If the fear, shame and hurt are big, you may go into a rage, which is anger that is out of control. People sometimes do scary things when they are enraged.

Sadness

This is the crucial emotion that lets you heal. In most cases, all you need when you are crying or feeling sad is someone to *listen*. You do not need someone to give advice or lecture. Neither children nor adults need others to fix or rescue them when they're feeling sad. What you need is someone who is grown-up enough to manage her own discomfort when you are sad, so that she doesn't squirm, avoid you or try to "make it all better" for you. Trying to make it all better for you is almost always the other person's way to shut down your sadness so that *she* doesn't feel uncomfortable anymore. Sadness *does* the healing all by itself, in most instances. In addition, research has proven that the ability to cry will help you maintain physical and mental health.

Joy/Pleasure

Joy and pleasure also help keep you physically and mentally healthy. Your "wants" are what determine who you are, and so joy is closely connected to your identity. In families where what you like is belittled or criticized, it is harder to form your own unique identity because you're always having to suppress or hide who you really are. "I want to paint my room blue" or "I like mystery novels" are statements of who you are. Thinking they are being helpful, others may say things like, "What do you want to paint your room *blue* for? Blue is a bad color for your room!" What they are really saying is "What moves your soul is not acceptable to me. Therefore, who you *are* is not acceptable to me." If this kind of response happens with any regularity, you will begin to disappear right before everyone's eyes.

Pain/Hurt

Pain warns you when you have been damaged, or when you are about to sustain damage, and so this is also crucial for your emotional and physical health. In families where pain is ignored, denied, minimized or belittled, children lose the information that is often critical for their survival. For example, if you minimize how painful an abusive relationship is and make excuses for horrible treatment from another, your life may be in danger. If you grow up in what we call a "pain denial family system," you may have a difficult time realizing how and why you keep getting into really painful situations. You won't have the crucial feedback that you need in order to extricate yourself from the pain. If your hand is burning on a hot stove, but you're in denial of your physical pain, you'll probably leave your hand there until it has third-degree burns on it. Pain is good. It helps you.

Shame

Shame lets you be accountable. Accountability lets you have humility. Humility helps you to be spiritual. Spirituality allows you to have healthy power. One definition of a perpetrator is someone who is shameless. Having high self-esteem does not mean that you have no shame. It means you have appropriate shame. Shame is the feeling that you are flawed—that you have defects—and all human beings have defects. All human beings feel some shame from time to time. When you can be embarrassed about those defects, you can change them. "I keep making sarcastic comments to people, thinking that it's cute or funny. But Joe Smith called me on it in front of everyone the other day, and I was really embarrassed. It hurt, too. At first I was really angry with Joe and wanted to lash out and get even, but now that I've thought about it for awhile, I think it's me who needs to change, not him. He was right." *That* is an example of healthy shame in action.

Psychologist Gershen Kaufman wrote that shame is the denial of your right to depend on others, so it has a lot to do with being "cut out of the herd" and with feeling "different."[15] When you are singled out as either *worse than others* or *better than everyone else,* you will often feel shame. Obviously, it will manifest itself differently if you're constantly told that you're better than everyone else is. In that case, you'll probably become arrogant, snooty, spoiled and narcissistic, which is the antithesis of humility and true power.

Guilt

Guilt is what lets you have a conscience, a moral sense, a sense of what's right and wrong. Guilt and shame often occur in the same moment. *Shame* tells you that you have a *defect inside* of yourself that you need to fix, such as impulsive anger that hurts others. *Guilt* is about your *behavior,* and tells you that you need to correct an action or right a wrong. It can take much longer and require more work to remove the defect that made you feel embarrassed than to right a wrong that you have done. The defect is inside of you and is part of you. The wrongdoing is outside.

Fear

Fear gives you wisdom. Being completely fearless means doing dumb things. Being courageous means doing scary things because they must be done, but knowing how scared you are when you do them. Watch the opening minutes of *Saving Private Ryan* and this will be clear. If you pretend you have no fear because it was shamed when you were little or because no one in your family acknowledged their fear in front of you, then you will continue to burn your hand on the same stove, or get hurt in the same kind of relationship, over and over again.

Loneliness

How could this be a positive emotion? Like wolves and apes, humans are social animals. By being social, the species has been able to survive on the planet longer than if we were roaming the planet alone, isolated from one another. The discomfort of loneliness propels us into groups, and we survive. Recent research shows that people with a good support system also live longer and fight serious disease much better than people who are emotionally isolated from others. If you're interested, read University of California cardiologist Dean Ornish's book *Love and Survival.* In it, he cites most of the major studies that show the powerful role our relationships play in our physical health.[16]

If you lack the unconscious rules that would make having complex relationships possible, then you will eventually create a shell around yourself so that you won't keep getting hurt. Unfortunately, the shell you create is the very thing that prevents further relationships, and so you become even more lonely and isolated. A negative spiral begins, and then you become stuck. To get out of this trap, you need to admit how lonely you are and then recognize that the loneliness is actually more harmful and painful than would be the hurt that comes from trying to make your relationships work.

Feeling Words That Fit
Under the Primary Categories

Safety/Warmth/Dependency—okay, comfortable, good, fine, relaxed, close, intimate, safe, supported, nurtured, cared-for, cared-about

Anger—mad, irritated, frustrated, ticked-off, crabby, rageful, infuriated, outraged, hostile, acrimonious, annoyed, vexed, resentful, wrath, indignant, combative, cruel, mean

Sadness—sad, depressed, blue, down, sorrowful, upset, disappointed, grieved, cheerless, gloomy, melancholy, dejected, despairing

Joy/Pleasure—happy, pleased, joyful, glad, excited, relieved, blissful, delighted, amused, thrilled, rapture, gratified, satisfied, euphoric, manic, proud

Pain/Hurt—suffering, hurt, pained, damaged, broken, agonizing, wounded,

Shame—ashamed, embarrassed, foolish, stupid, ugly, broken, damaged, "the bad seed," "the black sheep," defective, dirty, "the____one"

Guilt—guilty, contrite, culpable, responsible, "ought to," "shouldn't"

Fear—afraid, scared, anxious, nervous, tense, terrified, shocked, frightened

Lonely—isolated, lonely, separated, alienated, dissociated, alone, apart, distant, aloof, detached

We should point out that some of the words in the above list can fit under more than one primary category, such as "broken," which we list under both "hurt" and "shame." Also, if you look at all of the possible words in the dictionary that are used to describe feelings, each one is a combination of one or more of the primary ones. A complex feeling such as "disappointment" can be a mix of a couple of feelings, depending on the person and the situation. It might be a mix of sadness, shame and anger in one case. In another, it might be a mix of hurt, fear and shame.

Feel, Think, Act

Feelings are all normal and healthy, so don't let anyone tell you otherwise. *If someone says, "You don't feel sad, do you?" all you have to say is, "Yes, I do feel sad."* By not hooking into their shaming statement, you will make it easier for them to be ashamed of what they just said, and their shame will help them to be accountable and humble, and therefore more powerful.

Here's one of the most helpful reminders that we pass onto our clients. This is a sequence that in many cases is the best way to handle things that arise every day:

Feel ———> Think ———> Act

As we've learned already, feelings come first anyway. Something happens, the information goes to the limbic system of the brain, and then it radiates up into various regions of the cerebral cortex. Read Goleman's book if you want a detailed neurological explanation of this. What some people do, though, is become so dissociated from their feelings that they aren't aware of their emotions. They have the wrong emotional data on which to base a decision. So for all intents and purposes, this person will:

Think ———-> *Act* ———-> *Then Maybe Feel Later*

While this can be a good strategy when handling an emergency like a serious automobile accident, it's a poor way to have an emotionally intimate relationship with another.

When I feel, think and then act, it's as if my engine is running on all cylinders, not half of them. Here's an example. You're having a disagreement with a guy you've been going out with. All healthy couples fight. It isn't healthy to pretend that conflict isn't normal. He wants the relationship to become exclusive, but you aren't ready to do that. He says, "I need this to be an exclusive relationship. I've been hurt enough in past relationships." That's a pretty volatile statement, whether it's right or wrong. You may feel a mix of guilt about possibly hurting his feelings, shame that there may be something wrong with you for not wanting to commit yet, and fear that he may smother you and become controlling because of his own anxiety. You *could* overreact and say something angry or defensive that is driven by your fear, such as, "I can't be responsible for your past relationships. Life doesn't always work out the way we want it to. *You* need to grow up!" Or, you could feel, think about it and then act, in which case, you might calm yourself down first, and then say, "I understand that you've been hurt before. It's just that I'm not ready to make our relationship exclusive." What a huge difference: One response hurts both of you, while the other is respectful of both of you.

Learning to experience our feelings, to listen to what they are telling us, and then to *act appropriately* is the key to emotional intelligence. Feelings can be powerful at times. A panic attack, which is exaggerated fear, can make you feel like you're dying or going crazy. A shame attack can make you feel so small and isolated that you want to crawl under a rock and disappear. Emotional mastery is something that everyone must learn before they enter *psychological adulthood*. It isn't a matter of repressing and denying our feelings. It's a matter of *containing* them. To contain them means to feel them, but not let them run the show. *That's what it means for the dog to wag its tail, rather than the tail wagging the dog.*

6

Break the Silence:
It Takes *So Much Energy* to
Silently Scream

That which you bring forth will heal you.
That which remains hidden will destroy you.

—Anonymous

Your Parents Don't Know You

You are not alone if you feel that your parents don't know you. That's one of the more troubling patterns going on in families today. Many parents aren't around as much because of work and social commitments, and when they are, they don't seem to know how to connect with their kids. Many parents lecture instead of listen. It is an established fact that when anyone lectures in a face-to-face setting, the person being lectured to "zones out." This is true for adults as well as teenagers. Lecturing at someone is probably the most ineffective form of communication one can use. It has gotten to be such a problem that we even created a training video designed to help parents learn how to talk to kids (see "About the Authors" at the end of the book).

Recent research conducted by *Who's Who Among America's High School Students* demonstrates how uninformed many parents are. When asked if they thought high school students had problems with drinking, 41 percent of the students and 60 percent of the teachers thought so, but only 16 percent of the parents—parents of the top students in America's schools who were included in the survey—thought so! When parents were asked if their *own* kids had problems with alcohol, the estimate was 0.2 percent! The findings were similar when they were each asked about cheating. Of the teachers polled, 45 percent thought students cheated, 40 percent of the students admitted to cheating, but only 4 percent of parents thought their kids cheated! Most of the teenagers we've talked to over the past several years confirm these findings, too.

A *Newsweek* poll in May 1999 indicated that 90 percent of Americans say parents aren't spending enough time with their teenagers. In addition, 47 percent of Americans believe that very few parents really know what their teens are up to.[17] In *Ask the Children,* Ellen Galinsky noted that 56 percent of parents think that their children want more time with their parents, while only 10 to 15 percent of kids actually said they wanted more time with their parents. Apparently, it isn't more time with parents that kids crave, but rather *time that isn't hurried.* When asked if time with parents was rushed, 45 percent said that time with Mom is rushed, and 37 percent said that time with Dad is rushed. About one-third of the parents interviewed thought that their time with their kids was rushed.[18] Throughout *The 7 Worst Things (Good) Parents Do,* we continually emphasized how crucial it is for parents and children to have enough "downtime" together to connect with each other, share hopes and dreams, and listen to each other. Apparently many kids feel the same way.

Immediately after the Columbine shootings happened in Littleton, Colorado, in April of 1999, we went on countless TV and radio programs to add our two cents' worth to the discussions of how or why this could happen. As psychologists, we know that human beings *can't* shoot each other in cold blood without being dissociated—i.e., disconnected from themselves and others, "zoned out" in some way. Additionally, one's rage would have to be huge to plan and then carry out mass executions at one's high school. There would have to be a pretty big "disconnect" between those kids and their parents—some kind of intimacy problem in which the kids felt like no one was listening, or was even able to listen, for a long time. We also wondered what kind of parents would let their teenagers—the jocks in that high school—chronically and mercilessly tease other kids without severe consequences, the *least* of which would be removal from their sports teams.

Then in March 2000, we read an article in *USA Today*

summarizing a CBS *60 Minutes II* segment on some of the findings of the U.S. Secret Service regarding teenage school shooters. CBS correspondent Scott Pelley said that "Many of [these kids] were considering suicide seriously, and many of them say that what brought them to that point is malicious teasing in their school, which had gone on for a long time."[19] He added that most of them had shared some of their plans with classmates, and most of the teenage shooters who were interviewed said that they *"had no adult they could talk to."* We have been saying this for years, but we still find it unbearably sad.

One Teen's "Worst" List

The above facts are hard enough to hear. But we wondered how it felt at a personal level to be painfully, silently aware that the adults who are supposed to know you the best don't. A teenager in a small Midwestern town used the following words: lonely, scared, angry, lost. When asked to name one of the seven *worst* things teenagers do, she replied solemnly, "Silently scream." A couple of years later as she was leaving her teen years behind, we received the following from her, and with her permission we reproduce it here:

> *Here are the worst things that I did as a teenager. Many of my friends did them, too. The first one is silently screaming—not telling adults around you what you need from them, such as emotional support, guidance and direction; not*

*telling them what is going on in your life, i.e., not bringing
the truth out in the open, such as "I need help getting involved
in more appropriate groups and activities than I'm in now."*
The next one is taking on the world—*not getting emotional
or physical help when you need it; thinking you are so strong
you can get through anything or die in the fight, such as suffering from clinical depression and not seeking help, trying to
persevere through it on your own and taking bad risks to prove
your strength in mind and life.* The third one is ignoring
the inner voice—*which is your conscience, which sometimes
sounds like Mom's preaching or Dad's concern, but is really
your heart/moral judgment, which holds a lot of wisdom and
should be given the respect it truly deserves . . . respect shown
in listening and understanding, since it is your own heart and
conscience speaking. . . . You owe it to your own body, mind,
and soul to take it seriously. It affects the future of "you."*
Next is ignoring your own talents and interests for
another image, *which is pretty self-explanatory. For example,
I gave up the viola when we moved in the middle of my freshman year because I didn't know how the other kids would perceive it, and I wanted to be accepted. I regret that terribly.
And although I always liked writing and poetry, I gave it up
as I got into high school, just when I could have been developing it in the classroom, because I feared that it would not be
good enough academically. . . . It meant too much to me to risk
putting it out in the spotlight.* Next comes too much reliance
on friends, *not enough on family—relying too much on peer
support. You should be going to adults in your life fairly regularly for support as well. Although they may seem to be out
of touch at times, they have a lot more life experience and*

wisdom than even your most worldly-wise friends do. Regular support from competent adults in your life should allow you to become even more independent, stronger and wiser than peers who rely almost solely on each other.

What a wise young woman. She then went on to say that while some of the mistakes she made as a teenager were extremely painful, she was able to learn from them and correct them as her life got healthier each year. The turning point in her life occurred one day when, having gotten into some fairly serious trouble, the assistant principal of her high school looked her in the eyes and said to her, point-blank, "You know, *you don't have to do these things.*" He said it in such a matter-of-fact but engaging way, and she was so ready to move her life in a new direction, that it slipped right past her hurt, loneliness, anger and defensiveness. She said that from that day forward she was on a different path. We were intrigued when she said that she had found the ending of James Michener's novel, *Journey,* to be especially meaningful to her. *Journey* was actually part of Michener's original manuscript for his larger work, *Alaska.* After finishing this shorter-than-usual Michener novel, we could see why it meant so much to her. If you read it, *be sure to read every last page.*

We could be glib and smug in writing this book, except that we know better. It would be so easy to say, "Well, of course being a teenager is hard. It's the *sturm und drang*—the stress and strain—about which social scientists have written for decades. That's just the way teenagers are." For us to say that would be to trivialize two decades' worth of our own clinical work with *adults,* as well as teenagers, because the problem of "silently screaming" is not unique to teenagers. We all do it to some degree, and the more we do it, the more pain we experience in our lives.

You might wonder what teenager really wants help from adults. Whether you are a teenager or a middle-aged adult, you may think that adults are "the enemy," and that teenagers don't want adults *more* involved in their lives, they want adults *less* involved in their lives. Then in the next instant an image flashes through your brain, and you hear yourself say, "All people need to feel safe somewhere in their lives. All people need to feel that it's okay to depend on others from time to time." You would be correct on both counts.

There is nothing odd about wanting as much freedom as you can possibly get, and then moments later feeling gratefully relieved that you can't have everything you want. This isn't unique to teenagers. This is unique to *human beings.* We want it all, but know that it would kill us if we had it all. Human beings of any age feel ambivalent from time to time. You want to eat another piece of chocolate cake, but you don't. You want to go to your friend's party, but you have a feeling that there will be trouble there tonight, so part of you doesn't want to go. You'd like to call in sick for work today, but you want to get in and make some money because you're broke. This is pretty easy to comprehend, but somehow when a teenager experiences ambivalence about her life, everyone gets discombobulated. Adults who can't comprehend this ambivalence simply need to go back and do a bit of self-examination. Ambivalence is part of being human.

What *is* unique to being a teenager is that you don't just need to rely on others, you need to rely specifically on your parents or guardians. Therein lies the rub. If I need to rely on my parents for certain things like money or guidance, then I am in good shape if my parents are healthy and reliable. But if they aren't—and no parent is perfectly healthy nor perfectly reliable—then there will be times when I *need* to lean on my parents, but I will believe I can't because they aren't there physically or emotionally, or worse, because they are the ones hurting me. In these cases, I may believe that I have no safe option except to *silently scream while I am at home.* Our Midwestern teenager tried to tell her parents that she was floundering, but they weren't able to hear her—they were floundering in their own problems.

The problem then becomes one best described by so many teenagers: "I will have to make up some of my own rules as I go along. If I have to make up my own rules as I go along, I will invariably make some mistakes, and, on occasion, these mistakes could result in painful consequences." One of the solutions to this dilemma that many teenagers have used is to take a closer look at their own secrets, and then to find somewhere safe to share them, or at least parts of them.

I Have a Secret

Everybody has at least one big secret. Some people have more. The secrets may change or accumulate with age, but they are always there. One of the rewards of being practicing psychologists for so long is that we know from firsthand experience that every single person on the planet has something somewhere inside of them that they would be embarrassed to talk about to other human beings. To be trusted enough by people for them to share these secrets and unburden their hearts and souls with us is humbling.

Teenagers have secrets just like everyone else. Over the past twenty-five years, we have heard all of the following secrets and many more from teenagers.

1. My parents really like my boyfriend, but I have serious reservations. He's a nice guy, but I just don't think it's a good match. I'm afraid I'd be letting them down if I broke up with him because they seem *so* enthralled with him. It's wearing me out emotionally.

2. I have been drinking heavily for the past three years. I have managed to keep it completely hidden from my parents because I'm a straight-A student, on the student council and am a cheerleader, so I couldn't possibly be into drinking or drugs, right? Wrong. They are *so* naïve. They have no idea how deeply into it I am. Secretly, I am really angry with them for not seeing the real me.

3. I hate my father. I love him, too, but I feel so ignored by him that I get incredibly confused. I want to spend time with him, and then when we do, he constantly corrects me, excusing his criticism by saying, "I'm on you a lot because I care about you. You know that, don't you?" He says it in such a pathetic yet authoritarian way that my guts are in knots and I have no way to put words on how I feel. If I *did* tell him directly, it feels like he'd either be crushed or would try to

criticize me even more, so I just smile vacantly and hope that the knots go away by themselves someday.

4. I know a lot of kids at school and am very popular. My parents tell all their friends how great I am. They're so proud of how socially adept I am. If they only knew that I am constantly on the verge of tears. I'm just *waiting* for someone to discover that I'm a fraud. I have all these friends, but not one of them, nor any of my family members, know how insecure I am, and how fragile I feel right now. I'm afraid they'd be so shocked and disappointed if I *did* admit these feelings that they'd run in the other direction.

5. I would never tell anyone this because they'd probably either laugh at me or think I was crazy because who ever thinks of suburban middle-class families as desperately needing help? When I grow up, I want to help people who live in middle-class suburbs because from what I can tell they all seem to be so alienated, lonely, shallow and troubled. I don't know why I feel this way. I just know they need saving, and I'd like to be one of the ones who does it.

6. I am terrified of the dark, and *nobody* knows it. It's so embarrassing. I'm eighteen years old, and my heart pounds, my hands perspire profusely, and I shake whenever I am in the dark, especially if I'm by myself. I hide it gallantly, but it's a terrible fear to have.

7. I made a suicide plan two weeks ago.

8. I had sex with a college girl last weekend, and I'm only fourteen. I am really confused now. I mentioned it to a couple of buddies, and they thought it was cool.

I tried to explain that I was also ambivalent about it, and vacillated between being ashamed and guilty and being preoccupied and obsessed with her ever since, but they just chuckled, grinned, yucked it up and patted me on the back in congratulations. I just wanted someone to understand how I felt.

9. My parents fight *a lot*. Every two to three weeks they start fighting around 11:00 P.M. and the arguing escalates until around 1:00 A.M. or so, until they become physically violent. I try to fall asleep, but I also try to stay awake and listen to what they're saying because I'm terrified of their getting divorced. My older sister and I haven't told a soul. We just keep hoping things will get better. I'm not getting enough sleep. I'm tired.

10. I don't *want* to go to college. I want to go to a technical school, learn how to do carpentry, and then apprentice with someone until I become an expert at it. *Then* I may want to go back and go to college, but maybe not. Both of my parents insist that I apply to colleges. It's as if it's more important to them that I go than it is for me. It feels awful.

Who Do You Trust?

Once you've taken a look at what's beneath your own surface, the next challenge is to look around your world and try to determine who can be trusted with your secrets. There is actually a lot of skill and finesse involved here, some of which can only be gained by trial and error, which is the scary part. If I don't open up at all, my secrets may bury me, but if I share them with the wrong person, I could get hurt. Again, this isn't just a dilemma for teenagers. It's a dilemma for everyone.

Imagine a lost or wounded wild animal, a deer perhaps, that has wandered into your yard. You can see it is in distress, but as soon as you try to approach it so you can offer it some food or capture it so you can take it to the vet, it darts away. You're scared for it, and disappointed and sad as you see it wander off into the woods. The next morning, you look out into the yard and the deer is there again. It enters the yard very tentatively, clearly scared, but clearly on a mission, too. It is the walking embodiment of ambivalence. It senses the *possibility* of safety and comfort in your yard, but it has nothing to confirm that safety, so it wisely acts according to its fear. It is this waffling between safety and danger, between feelings of comfort and fear, that causes such intense ambivalence.

As this drama unfolds in your backyard, what becomes clear to you is that both you and the deer are *controlling the outcome—you each play your part.* You both want something, and getting it depends on your wisdom in knowing when to move forward and when not to, your risk-taking ability, and how much restraint and patience you can muster at critical moments in the drama. The same is true of the deer. If all of these elements are in sync, a relationship between you and the deer will unfold. If it does, you can be assured of one thing: Neither of you will get 100 percent of what you're after because that is, by definition, the nature of a good relationship. It is a dance between two autonomous creatures who each have the power to stay or leave. The deer befriends you, but never lets you get close enough to capture her and take her to the vet. You accept that you have gotten this close and that the deer will heal, but not as perfectly as you might have wished. Everybody wins.

Friends

So, whom can you trust? Teenagers share a lot of things with each other, which is good. Being able to open up with people who may be going through very similar circumstances is a powerful source of comfort in life. Dr. David Spiegel of Stanford University wondered how important this kind of peer support was in mediating disease, so he worked with two groups of women who had metastasized breast cancer. One group of terminally ill women received standard medical care. The other group received standard medical care plus participation in a therapy group twice a week. The women in the therapy group shared their pain, sorrow, joy and laughter with each other, which is a very intimate thing to do if you're dying. These women lived twice as long as the women in the other group—thirty-seven months as opposed to nineteen months.[20]

What we have learned from the men's and women's therapy groups that we have been running since the early 1980s is that it is the simple structure and safety that we provide as therapists that seems to be the most important thing that we can do. The rest is up to the group members.

With an average stay of around eighteen months (some stay for a shorter time, some as long as three to four years), what happens after awhile is just like you and the deer in your backyard. Each person gradually learns that it is safe to share feelings, problems and personal secrets. They also learn what is safe for them to share and what isn't. An amazing amount of healing and growth happens when people sit together for a couple of hours each week with the expressed purpose of sharing the details of their lives with each other. It is truly remarkable.

Adults

Sharing things with friends is essential. Emotional isolation from one's peers can be one of the most stressful things a person can experience. However, as we noted at the beginning of this chapter, teenagers are hungry for understanding, support and guidance from adults, too. In our first book, *Adult Children: The Secrets of Dysfunctional Families,* written in 1988, we used the "cup metaphor" to explain how people choose intimates, especially deeper relationships like romantic partners. The truth conveyed by this metaphor is that we each unconsciously pick partners who are equal to us in terms of health and dysfunction, whether we believe it or not, and whether we consciously wanted to or not.

We Always Pair Up with Our Emotional Equals

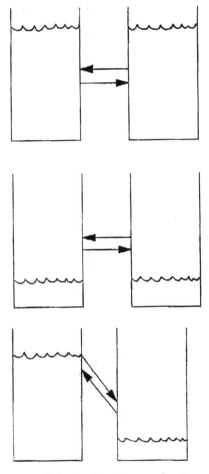

These Two Wouldn't Get Past the Second Date

Emotional Health and Partner Choice

When it comes to picking people in whom we can confide, this is particularly important to know. If we are in over our heads and we try to figure it out with the help of our closest friends, it is very possible that they will be just as lost as we are. You might say, "But they aren't lost in the same way," and that could be true, but if your cup is one-third full and so is your friend's, we suspect that you'll both be lost in the midst of your problem in no time.

Here is a classic example: Let's say you are addicted to alcohol or drugs and your best friend doesn't use at all, but is just as confused in other ways. Your best friend talks to you when you're drunk. She covers for you when you get in the car and drive away while drunk. She nags you and pleads with you to get professional help, but when you give an intellectualized but nonsensical reason why you won't get professional help, she continues to go back and forth with you, for months and months. If she were healthier than you were, she'd dial 911 when you drive away drunk, and would be strong enough and have enough support from her family and other friends to be able to withstand your temporary anger at her. (People who get treatment for their addictions usually wind up thanking the friends who "turned them in" once they get better, even though they "hated them" bitterly right afterwards.)

The ability to seek out others who are wiser or more competent than us in certain areas of life is one of the characteristics that clearly separates healthy, emotionally powerful people from those who remain mired in their own problems. In our line of work, therapists who aren't willing to receive advice on their cases from other therapists are viewed as dangerously flawed. The reluctance or inability to seek help from those wiser or more competent than oneself has long been seen as a typical characteristic of an adult who grew up in a painful home. This is because in painful families we learn that it isn't safe to rely on anyone but ourselves. It's one of those unconscious rules that we pick up and carry into adulthood, where like a nasty computer virus, it operates in the background, making personal and relationship happiness or career success extremely elusive.

As our Midwestern teenager told us so eloquently, finding adults with whom you can share your problems is essential. There is no peer substitute for the wisdom that someone wiser and more competent can provide us. The problem with this is that the adults with whom we *should* be able to talk candidly are not always available. As scary as it might seem in some families, it is usually worth the risk to at least try to talk to your parents about what you need or what is bothering you. Remember that it is not your job to raise your parents or to pretend that everything is "fine" in order to protect your parents from discomfort. We have found that with kids and parents being so overextended, it is often enough for you to stop, look your parents in the eye, and set out some *listening ground rules,* something like, "Dad, Mom, I need you to sit down for just a minute and *listen* to me. I just want you to *listen.* I don't need you to fall apart, I don't need you to wring your hands in despair, and I don't need you to tell me what to do or to analyze me. I just need you to *listen.*" When we work with adults on things like this, they will actually write out and rehearse what they want to say so that the chances of getting tongue-tied are diminished.

There are some specific situations in families that make this kind of disclosure to parents difficult. If you've really tried to get through to your parents as outlined above and it just doesn't seem to be working, then you may have to go to Plan B, which is to find someone else to talk to. Some of the *parental impediments to sharing risky things* are briefly listed below. Remember: Just because these may be present to some degree does not mean that you can't rely on your parents. Sometimes taking the time and the risk to state the *listening ground rules* does the trick.

Some Parental Impediments to Sharing Risky Things

1. Parents who seem to need you more than you need them. Pat Love's *The Emotional Incest Syndrome* covers this problem brilliantly.
2. Parents who need you not to struggle or be in pain because they haven't yet learned to be comfortable with feelings or the fact that part of life is just plain painful.
3. Parents who flat-out don't care (these are extremely rare).
4. Parents who are so mean, critical or abusive that there don't seem to be ways to enter safely into a risky discussion.
5. Parents who are so seriously addicted or mentally ill that their troubles are literally overwhelming them, leaving no room for you.

How Do You Test the Waters?

Whether it's with your parents, a teacher, school counselor, coach, minister or priest, friend's parent or other adult, there is a way to be like that deer in the woods who enters the backyard so tentatively at first. A lot of you already know how that works. You're riding in the car with Dad and as matter-of-factly as you can, you say, "I was reading that article in the paper about domestic violence this morning. It was pretty interesting. Did you read it?" In chess, this might be similar to "an opening gambit." In being a teenager who would like some support or guidance from her father, it's called "testing the waters" or "sending up a trial balloon" because even after you say it there are several directions in which *you* can still steer the conversation. For example, if your Dad is really good at feelings and relationships, he'll go slowly, too, just in case. He might reply, "Yes, I did. It was written very well and had a lot of good points. What impressed you about the article?"

"Well," you continue, "I didn't realize how many bright, competent, powerful women were the victims of domestic violence. That surprised me, I guess."

Dad says, "Yes. It doesn't have much to do with IQ or financial success. It's much more common than most people know. I'm glad people are getting more comfortable talking about it."

Now it's time to take your cue. "It made me think a little bit about my relationship with Phil. I mean, he's never hit me or anything, but sometimes he gets so angry at other drivers on the freeway that I'm afraid he might do something stupid someday."

Now, contrary to what some parents do, it's Dad's turn to back off and *listen* and affirm, *not* give advice or lecture or become overly anxious. If he were to do any of those, he'd scare you back into the woods. "Yeah. I had a friend like that once. It took me a long time to admit I was just plain scared to ride in the car with him. Do you get scared sometimes?"

"Yeah," you say, tentatively. "So, how did you handle it with your friend?"

"It didn't turn out like I'd hoped. I asked him very politely if he'd not do that when I was in the car because it really made me nervous."

"And?"

"And he must have felt really embarrassed because he launched into a tirade and yelled about what a wimp I was."

"What did you do?"

"I was confused for a couple of days, so I talked it over with some of my other friends, and finally with my parents. After that, I just decided never to ride in the car with him again. By the way he kept teasing me when I turned down his offers to drive, I'm not sure he ever really got it, but that didn't matter. I never rode with him again. And he never had an occasion to scare me with his uncontrollable anger again."

"Hm-m-m-m-m," you say. Then after a comfortable silence you add, "Thanks, Dad. I have some things to think about here."

"You're welcome, honey."

Testing the waters *is* just like the interaction with the deer in the woods. This includes the conclusion, which is never 100 percent of what you wanted (the perfect answer that would insure that you could stay with Phil and not be subjected to his rage anymore), and never 100 percent of what Dad might have wanted (to completely protect his daughter from the struggles in life). Thus, you both win.

Isn't life interesting? The paradox is that the very thing we need to do to make ourselves healthier is the thing we fear the most—in this case, opening ourselves up to someone else. The solution to the paradox is fairly simple: *Never give up.*

7

Get Healthy Power:
Learn to Respectfully
Make Things Happen

It is not ill-bred to adopt a high manner
with the great and powerful,
but it is vulgar to lord it over humble people.

—Aristotle, *The Nicomachean Ethics,* c. 340 B.C.

What happens when you assemble a bunch of "losers," as some would call them, take them seriously and teach them the principles of behavior modification so that they can have some power over their school environment? In the early 1970s, Harry Rosenberg, director of special education for the school district in Visalia, California, began an amazing research project in one of the junior high schools.

He and his consultant, psychologist Paul Graubard, didn't pick just any junior high school, either. They picked the one in the district that had the worst reputation and the worst record for integrating special education students into regular classes. The school had the highest suspension and expulsion rates in the district, and it was the most likely to label kids "incorrigible."

One fourteen-year-old in the study terrified his eighth-grade teachers because he weighed 185 pounds and was the school's best athlete, but was also vicious and violent. He knocked out other students, earned a forty-day suspension for hitting a principal with a stick, and had been arrested and put on probation for two-and-a-half years for assault. In other words, the kids in this study were not the cream of the crop. By the end of the study, this violent eighth-grader was saying things like, "You really help me learn when you're nice to me," to his math teacher. He was also hanging around after class to chat with his teachers.

Back in the 1970s, demonstration projects like this were going on all over the country as part of an epidemic of enthusiasm for psychology's hot new technology. It was being used in homes, classrooms, mental hospitals, prisons, corporations, you name it. What was "it"? It is behavior modification. Although the principles used have been around ever since we earned the right to be called *Homo sapiens,* what turned this set of principles into a technological revolution was the work of psychologist B. F. Skinner, inventor of the famous, or infamous, Skinner Box. He took a very basic fact of life—that living organisms tend to seek rewards and avoid punishments—and devoted his entire career to systematically observing all the factors that come into play as people and animals go about seeking rewards and avoiding punishments.

Skinner made some fascinating discoveries along the way, some of which are just common sense, and many of which prove that until it's proven, the "common sense" you operate by could be nothing more than harmless superstition at the very least or, at the very worst, a hideously destructive myth. For example, how about this one: "Kids need to be punished regularly, and a good whipping strengthens them, helps them learn to deal with adversity, and teaches them to respect their parents." Wrong. Systematic behavioral research proves that (1) *realistic consequences* (you violate curfew, you don't get to use the car tomorrow night) that are (2) *enforced consistently* (absolutely no giving in to whining, begging, nagging, conning, manipulating), where there are a (3) *small number of reasonable rules* (rather than an endless list of unreasonable, picayune, unenforceable rules designed to make everyone, including parents, totally miserable) (4) produces happy children and teenagers who clearly *respect* and even *like* their parents. Whipping children teaches them to fear and avoid their parents, teaches them to become violent later on, teaches them to give up and fail all the time, teaches them to fear and therefore hate other adults and sets them up for a lifetime of misery.

This may all be obvious now, but it certainly wasn't just a few decades ago. From what our clients tell us, there are plenty of parents out there who are still trying to raise their kids with severe punishment, including psychologists who know this stuff inside and out academically, but who can't seem to use it in their daily lives. This is why social science can be so valuable, even if it appears to be boring at times. Perhaps Skinner's greatest single contribution to this branch of psychology was his emphasis on the need for people to be *systematic* if they wanted their behavior change efforts to succeed. This painstaking approach excited so many people for so long because it worked so well. In the next few paragraphs, we will briefly describe the most important parts of setting up such a program. As you read them, think of how you might use this as a way to have some healthy control over your world.

Define Behavior Clearly

Being systematic begins with *clearly defining* the behavior you want to change, which can be a challenge in itself. You can't say "I want my math teacher to treat me better" because that is such a vague goal that no one could measure it, and therefore no one could *consistently* reward it. What you think is "better" often conflicts with what the teacher or other students think is "better." It's much too vague. If you would like your math teacher to treat you better, you'll have to define "better." Successful managers and leaders know this one very well—if your employees don't know what's expected of them, they won't be able to perform, and that will be the manager's fault. Therefore, to say, "I would like my math teacher to look at me, make eye contact, and say 'good morning' once every other day, before class is over," is much closer to the mark.

Get a Baseline Measure

This is the first seemingly tedious, but absolutely crucial step in the process. People who don't have much patience or who are not yet ready for mature, systematic thinking will have to struggle with this one. Before you try to modify any behavior, you really need to find out how often it occurs naturally. This can be especially important when there is no longer a problem, but you still think there is. It is a well-researched fact that kids who cause trouble in school get labeled "troublemakers," and the label sticks. Even after these kids have turned around almost completely, many teachers will still see them as troublemakers. The same is true for adults. It takes time and repetition before a change in an adult's behavior is consistently recognized and appreciated.

You might be surprised when you measure your teacher's "morning greeting behavior" and discover that he does indeed make eye contact every once in awhile, although not nearly as much as he frowns and looks grumpy. Establishing a baseline measure of behavior is essential. If you would like to modify your teacher's reactions to you, then you'll need to know how often these things happen on their own. If they never happen, then you'll know that for certain after one to two weeks of baseline recording. If they happen once in a blue moon, you'll know that, too.

Establish Effective Consequences

Here is where many people sabotage the behavior change program they're setting up. An effective consequence is operationally defined. This means it is an effective consequence if it strengthens the behavior that it follows, i.e., if it works, it works, and if it doesn't, stop using it. While this may sound like a no-brainer, it isn't. It is very easy for adults and teenagers to *assume* that something is reinforcing when, in fact, it isn't. If you're spoiled and indulged so that your every whim and wish is satisfied immediately, money will probably not be a useful reinforcer for you. If deep down inside your algebra teacher really does care what others think of him and of his teaching abilities, then it may very well be reinforcing to him if you go up and say, "I can see that you're really a good algebra teacher. I sometimes act like I don't care because it's so hard for me to get it. I wonder if you'd be willing to help me a little bit after class." Figuring out what consequences will probably work is a challenging part of the process, and to do so it helps to use your creativity and emotional intelligence.

Apply the Consequence and Measure What Happens

After all this preliminary work is done, you're ready to modify the chosen behavior. There was a classic classroom experiment—some would call it a stunt—done by students at a major U.S. university and then replicated by impish students for years afterwards. The key to this experiment is that teachers really do care what students think about them. It's hard enough trying to prepare college classes week after week. It's even harder to get up in front of a bunch of students every day knowing that you'll be evaluated by them at the end of the semester and that your job and life will depend on their evaluations. Even if their job didn't depend on it, most teachers care deep down inside because that's human nature.

The only additional procedure you'll need to know about in order to understand this student experiment is what Skinner called *shaping.* Most people are familiar with how this works, even if they aren't always systematic about it. Skinner began his research by putting a rat in a box that had a lever and a food dispenser on one wall. He then began shaping the rat closer and closer to the goal behavior, which was to press the lever to get food. Using only behaviors that are normal for rats, like walking, turning, getting up on their haunches, exploring and pawing at things, Skinner began by dispensing a food pellet whenever the rat even *faced* the wall with the lever and dispenser on it. When the rat did this well, then he only rewarded the rat if it came within a few inches from the lever. Then, he only rewarded the rat if it got up on its haunches and sniffed the lever. *Then,* the rat finally hit the lever as part of its exploring process, and the food was dispensed immediately. From that moment on, the rat knew that if it wanted food, all it had to do was press the lever.

Shaping is very clever. This is the same procedure that animal trainers use to get porpoises to do all of their amazing tricks at Sea World, or that you may already have used while training your own dog. Skinner got so good at doing this that he even had some test projects in which pigeons inside of a U.S. Air Force missile would direct it to a target by pecking on a picture of the target fed to it via a camera!

We're sure you can think of all kinds of uses for *shaping*. What the students did was to try to gradually shape their professor so that by the end of the experiment, he would be teaching, motionless, from one corner of the room! So, using the exact same procedure as we just described above, they chose as their reinforcer their own interest in what the professor was saying. Every time he moved even an inch toward the corner of the room, the students would look up, pay attention to what he was saying, take notes and look interested. Every time he moved in the other direction, they'd look bored, doodle in their notebooks and look away or down.

Needless to say, it wasn't too long before that professor was teaching almost entirely from that corner of the room, which delighted the students to no end! As we said earlier, students in psychology classes all over the country have replicated that little classroom demonstration for years. The real trick to it, though, is for us to think of more practical uses of this behavioral technology, and to make sure that how we're using it is ethical.

After you have determined what consequence you'll use to reinforce your teacher to smile and say "good morning," then you apply that consequence and measure the number of times it happens in a week or month. The consequence— the reward—may be your smiling at him and saying something congenial or complimentary, like "I like that tie," or "Your lecture yesterday was really clear. I was able to do the math problems much better last night." If you are reading this and groaning that this is just *way too corny* for words, we encourage you to locate a copy of that article in *Psychology*

Today that describes the project in the Visalia school. It is truly remarkable how powerful *and* happy those students became once they realized that *they* could actually control how their teachers treated them.

Using What You Learn to Improve Your Own Life

Harry Rosenberg and Paul Graubard taught this very powerful technology to a bunch of "problem" junior high school kids, with amazing results. We put the word "problem" in quotation marks because one of the basic tenets of the behaviorists back then was that there really is no value in labeling people that way. A pure behaviorist wouldn't say that someone was a juvenile delinquent. He'd say that all kids want the same things whether they live in a wealthy suburb or the inner-city: respect, attention, clothes, to name a few. He would say that this particular kid lacks the behaviors needed to get what he wants in a socially appropriate way, and so our job is to simply help him learn those behaviors. That's exactly what Rosenberg and Graubard did, and it worked almost flawlessly.

There are no perfect technologies and no single solution to major social problems. We'll gladly say that behaviorism has been overused and overpraised since the 1960s. Many people feel overwhelmed by the amount of chaos in their lives. They feel helpless when it comes to having any sort of impact on their own lives. With this in mind, we will say that dusting off an "old" technology that might just give some of us a way to meet our needs in socially appropriate ways, instead of in violent hurtful ways, might be worth a shot. If you were to practice this stuff, even get one of your teachers to help you do a demonstration project using it, think of the possibilities. Think of all the ways you could use what we've just outlined above to help yourself or your fellow students improve the quality of your lives. Think of what a difference it would make if we saw ourselves as simply needing to learn some new skills, rather than as perpetual losers and outcasts.

Can you imagine how things might be different at home if you could figure out what reinforced your parents' behavior, and then used that knowledge in a positive way to improve how you got along? If you just picked one thing—cleaning your room, cleaning the bathroom you use, getting the mail, taking out the garbage, feeding the dog—and then did it *consistently and without having to be asked and without telling anyone that you're doing it,* we guarantee you that it will have a profound effect on how your parents treat you. You'd have to figure out a couple of their behaviors you'd like to monitor, like how many compliments your parents give you or how often they smile at you. You'd want to get a baseline measure first. Then you'd want to keep measuring after you start doing that one thing consistently. It would be just like those students in that school in Visalia, California. *You* would be controlling the outcomes by doing something that you thought through ahead of time.

Using a more systematic approach like this gives people power. If you assume for a moment that we *do* all want the same things, in general, and that some of us just don't know how to get those things appropriately, then *taking charge, seizing the initiative, seeing ourselves as having some mastery and control over our environment* will be far more powerful than getting stuck in the victim or perpetrator roles. Remember Myrtle Faye Rumph in South Central L.A. Many of the otherwise successful adults with whom we work have power problems because they haven't figured out how it works. They either take what they want, when they want it, until everyone in their life leaves them (perpetrator); or they are too fearful to risk looking foolish, or being criticized, or unloved, and thereby hardly ever go after what they want or need (victim).

Adults who tend to get stuck in the victim role will sometimes bypass a powerful and relatively simple solution and opt for a reaction that ultimately makes things worse. Sometimes the best thing to do is to appeal to an authority figure, like the police or the courts. Sometimes it makes a lot more sense to either drop your complaint altogether or to strike a compromise. If you have a dispute with a moving company, for example, you could sue them, but it had better be a pretty big lawsuit because by the time you're done your legal fees could easily exceed any settlement the court might award. Adults who were treated poorly when they were children have more of a tendency to want to fight everyone and everybody about every little dispute. In fact, this is one of the common symptoms of having grown up in a painful family. Teens living in painful families often do the same thing.

Some Power Suggestions

In this next section, we are going to offer you some suggestions and examples of powerful action. We are offering these with the very clear awareness that what could be powerful in one situation or for one person in one situation may not be powerful at all in a different situation or for a different person. In other words, there is no simple straightforward formula for demonstrating healthy power. Also, in many situations the difference between being powerful and being ineffective may be a look, a glance, a turn of a phrase, one's tone of voice, the level of confidence you feel when speaking, and so forth. A lot of it depends on how you execute the maneuver, which is why learning from someone who is older, wiser and more experienced can make a big difference.

Power at Home, School or Work

Management consultant Charlotte Beers shared some of her wisdom on *Good Morning America* one November morning in 1999. Specifically, she shared three excellent strategies for becoming more successful at work, especially in a corporate culture where it's easy to become invisible and powerless. As you digest these three strategies, consider why we think these are such good suggestions for people who want to gain power in any setting where competence is valued. We would also ask you to consider how these three can be applied in a family, a clique, a classroom or a committee at school.

Speak Up

People who stay in the background stay in the background! This isn't about introversion versus extraversion, either. Successful introverts—the majority of CEOs of Fortune 500 companies are introverts, by the way—let their ideas be known. Can you imagine Bill Gates not speaking up? This is about making your presence known. It's about sticking your neck out. It's about finding your voice.

For example, in the article about the Visalia study, Rosenberg and Graubard also told of a sixth-grade student named Peggy. The other kids constantly teased Peggy despite the fact that she was attractive and intelligent. They helped Peggy design a behavior modification program to change the students' attitudes towards her. They asked Peggy to pick three classmates that she would like to have as friends, and then taught her what to do. Peggy said, "I ignored Doris if she said anything bad to me. But when she said anything nice to me, I'd help her with her work, or compliment her, or sit down and ask her to do something with me."[21] Peggy's results were described as "spectacularly successful."

There have been countless studies looking at how men and women communicate in the workplace, such as Deborah Tannen's *You Just Don't Understand.* Most of the studies support the fact that men are much more aggressive and forceful in meetings. They'll jump in and blurt out what they have to say even if they have to interrupt someone else. They'll monopolize the floor more and longer. They're just more competitive. Women tend to be less aggressive in meetings. They fear hurting others' feelings and therefore don't interrupt as much, and, in general, are simply more polite than men. What all of that means is that if women want to make it in the work world, they'll have to learn how to have power. It doesn't mean they have to be as pushy as men are, either. It simply means that women have to find a way to be heard, to command attention, to take the floor and speak until they've said their piece.

This struggle to be heard isn't confined to women, though. Many of us, maybe even most of us, have trouble being assertive in group settings, exerting our own influence (i.e., power) in groups, and making our ideas and wishes known. If you add shyness to the mix, it becomes even harder to do. But male or female, shy or bold, extravert or introvert, it is each person's job to stick up for herself or himself.

Become an Expert at One Thing

The larger the organization and the more complex the task, the more likely it is that there will be things that fall through the cracks. That's just the nature of systems. If you're the only one in the group who knows how to draw things accurately, either because you already knew how to do it or because you chose to get some help and *become* that expert, then you have a niche that you can claim as your own. It is easier to build an identity or a presence within a group if you can position yourself in a way that is unique.

Have Unstoppable Curiosity

We love this one. You may or may not be familiar with the characteristics of people who grew up in alcoholic families, but one of the common traits is a "fear of looking stupid" which leads to a strong attitude of "I'd rather do it myself." You might think this stems from independence, but it is actually driven by unhealthy shame: "If I have to ask people how to do it or where to find it, they'll think I'm weak."

Our clients who grew up in alcoholic or abusive homes recall poignant but humorous stories around this problem. One man recalled the day he stood in front of rows and rows of hooks and fasteners in the hardware store trying to figure out which one would be right for attaching something to a concrete block wall. After what seemed like hours, he picked one out and bought it. When he tried to install it, he discovered that it was the wrong type of fastener. With his tail between his legs, he went back to the hardware store, mustered up all the courage he could, then asked the store manager which fastener to use. The manager was delighted to be of some help, and the man was on his way in a matter of minutes.

That man said his life began to change after that because he started to watch other adults around him, especially the successful ones, to see what they were doing when it came to asking questions. He admitted that he'd never noticed before because he'd never been looking for the behavior before, but what he observed was that the *most successful and powerful* people he knew *asked questions all the time.* After that, the man said that he really had to struggle to reconstruct his own internal framework regarding dependency, power, success and shame.

His old framework said that if he asked questions or asked for help, (1) he'd possibly be belittled because that's what his father did to him when he was a kid. At the very least, (2) he'd be admitting that he was temporarily in a "one-down" position, which could be interpreted as a sign of weakness, or (3) he'd be admitting that he was dependent on others, and he'd vowed not to be dependent on anyone from the time he was a little boy. He couldn't rely on his family to make life safe for him then, so why should he rely on anyone now? If this sounds all confused and convoluted, we ask you to struggle with it for awhile because it is one of the most common mistaken belief frameworks that keeps people stuck, unhappy and, yes, powerless.

The new framework that he began to construct from the inside out said (1) I learned it wrong because when I was a child in my family I had no other reference point. It made sense to believe what I believed back then because *in my family, with my scary father, it was true.* (2) As I look at the competent, successful people around me, what I see is that they are continually asking questions, letting themselves be vulnerable, temporarily being "one-down." It's the only way to acquire information, and information or knowledge is ultimately power. Furthermore, I see that these people I now watch (3) have an almost innocent, open, childlike curiosity about the world. They take a genuine interest in how other people view things, how other people solve problems, and in the inventions and creations of others. Because of this interest in others, (4) I see that others are drawn to people like this. People *like* us when we are open and take an interest in them. Therefore, (5) I now know that I can increase my effectiveness, competence and power by asking questions and having unstoppable curiosity.

Power in Romantic Relationships

"My boyfriend is a nice guy. I feel uncomfortable saying this, but actually my boyfriend is too nice. He constantly says stuff like, 'Whatever you want to do is fine with me,' and 'I don't care. I'm easy to please.' It makes me mad, and when I get mad I feel so *guilty* because he never gets mad back. My last boyfriend was scary. I don't want *that* again, but this isn't working, either."

It is very important to have power in our relationships, and this is never as important as in our closest ones. In fact, the struggle to balance power in romantic relationships is one way to summarize what determines whether a couple will "make it" or not. If one person must constantly dominate the other, there really *is* nothing upon which to base love because, by definition, this kind of love is supposed to be mutual. In relationships where one person always yields to the other, the energy—the very life force—in the relationship gradually fizzles until there's no relationship at all. If you have ever been at either extreme of this continuum, and most of us have, you know it doesn't feel right to always have your own way, nor does it feel right to give in all the time. Our ongoing efforts to keep the power balanced are what keep relationships from getting stale.

"I want to go to a movie tonight."

"Oh, shoot. I'm not really in the mood for a movie. I'd like to go over to Sue's house. Some of our friends are meeting there to watch videos."

"I've spent so much time with them lately, and we haven't had any time alone."

"But Pam and Jennifer are going to their mom's for most of the rest of the summer. I won't get to see them again until August."

"You just saw them last night! And you said good-bye to them then!"

"I know, but I really want to go to Sue's and watch videos."

"I don't."

This conversation is now at the point of balance, but is about to do what pilots call "going into a stall." To avoid the stall, one or the other will have to yield; or they will both have to pour more energy into it until it heats up and forces a resolution.

"You are so *possessive!* You just want to own me!"

"You must be kidding! Why would I want to do that? You're so selfish and self-centered! I can't believe how self-centered you are. You *always* get your way!"

"Hah! You *must* be kidding!"

"This isn't about you wanting to go to Sue's to say good-bye to Pam and Jennifer! This is about you wanting to get your way. Your parents are nice, but they spoil you!"

"All right! That's it! When you insult my family, that's enough! I'm out of here!"

"Good! Have a great time!"

"I will!" She slams the door behind her and storms out to her car.

"What a brat," he mutters to himself. "I need some space from her."

The above interchange may be perfectly healthy, and may be a sign that this relationship has a chance of lasting quite a bit longer; or it may mean that the relationship is just about over. Taken by itself, there isn't enough information to know. *Is* she spoiled? If so, is she ready to grow up some more? *Is* he possessive and, therefore, needy? If so, is *he* ready to grow up some more? Do they *both* need to grow, or do they just need some breathing room—some room to be separate—and this disagreement simply serves to give them some of that?

Relationships are made up of thousands of negotiations like the one above in which your needs and your partner's needs collide and combine to either ultimately bring you closer together or eventually bring the end of the relationship. Being able to assert your power in a relationship must be balanced with the ability to compromise and respect your partner's power. Being able to express healthy, clear, *non-abusive anger* is necessary to having an enduring relationship. Being able to compromise, yield and appreciate the needs and wants of your partner are equally important. Trying to balance those in yourself, and between you and the other person, is one of several things that make a relationship healthy.

The Power to Make Friends and Fit In

One of the most important skills that many kids learn in their families is how to fit in with and get along with other people. This is exciting because there has been enough concrete research by psychologists like John Gottman at the University of Washington, Steven Asher at the University of Illinois, Bernardo Carducci at Indiana

University Southeast and John Lochman at Duke University to define how kids manage to fit in. We also know how to teach kids to do it if they didn't learn it in their homes. It's a teachable skill, in other words. Whenever something is shown to be teachable, it means that it isn't a permanent trap that you're in. It's simply a problem with a solution.

Kids who seem to fit in well with others have learned certain skills from their parents that Daniel Goleman included in his definition of emotional intelligence: (1) These kids take an interest in other kids instead of being too focused on their own anxiety or performance. They ask other kids questions and pay attention to what other kids say and do. They go out of their way to say something positive to other kids. After all, deep down inside, everybody likes a compliment now and then. (2) These kids are aware of their own feelings, so that their feelings do not unconsciously get in the way of interactions. (3) They are also good at dealing with conflict in ways that cool things down rather than heat them up. We all know people who are good at doing this without being "wimpy" or weak. It's a matter of remaining in charge of the interaction at the same time that you're helping to turn down the heat. You can say something like "I can see your point, yes. That makes sense to me," or "We could go to the movie you want to see today, and then go to the one Bob wants to see tomorrow. Would that work?"

As you might have guessed, they also (4) tended to perceive things in a more positive light than did kids who had a harder time fitting in. When you come from a painful family, you often learn to protect yourself from very real threats—either verbal or physical. This sets you up to perceive more things as threatening than there actually are. For example, when someone accidentally bumps into you in a crowded mall, is it *always* because they are rude, is it *sometimes* because they are rude, or is it *usually* because it was so crowded that the person didn't see you and didn't mean to bump into you? How you perceive others' behaviors can have a powerful bearing on how you fit in with kids at school. In the Visalia study, the kids were very accurate at identifying negative teacher behavior, but they actually had to be trained to accurately identify positive teacher behavior because they routinely misperceived a teacher's positive comments as "chewing them out"!

Learning to have healthy power in social situations is incredibly important, which is why it is so exciting for us to watch others acquire that power during their therapy. In our clinical practice, we have found the same things as the psychology literature reports to be true: Even people with severe social anxiety disorder are able to overcome their symptoms if they are willing to face increasingly complex social situations and learn "the tricks of the trade" along the way.

8

Face the Serious Stuff: Some Things Are Too Big to Keep Buried

Often the test of courage
is not to die, but to live.

—Vittorio Alfieri, *Oreste,* IV, c. 1785

Listening Rather Than Lecturing

You have to study harder! Don't you want to get into a good college? Do you want to wind up in a dead-end job like my good-for-nothing uncle? My uncle has a near-genius IQ, but he frittered away his childhood screwing around in school, goofing off, making a joke of everything, and now look at him! What a loser! If you don't study harder, you're going to amount to nothing when you grow up, just like him. Hey! *Look at me* when I'm talking to you! Look at me! Why do you do that? Why do you always look away when I'm talking to you? That's what I mean. You can't even look me in the eye when I'm talking to you. Now listen to me! Pay attention!"

Who could, or would even *want* to, listen to a tirade like that? Especially when the words spewing out of Dad's mouth are so mean? His fear of your failing in life may be genuine and well-intentioned deep down inside, but the way in which the message is conveyed is so unfortunate. If he *wanted* to set you up for failure, he couldn't have picked a better way to do it than to give you that kind of lecture. There is another kind of lecture that may be less overtly painful, but it is still a lecture and will rarely achieve the intended result. In this one, Dad may speak in a calm, almost flat, monotonic voice, droning on and on as your eyes glaze over, you squirm in your seat, and you pray for someone or something to interrupt the monologue.

Giving someone a face-to-face lecture does *not* work. It is curious that despite its ineffectiveness, parents do it to children, children do it to parents, parents do it to other adults, and teenagers do it to each other, especially when they are worried about each other. Even though it has been shown to be the *least effective* way to help someone learn something, it is still one of the most common ways that people try to intervene in each other's lives.

With the above said, the question we had to keep asking ourselves when we considered writing this chapter was:

"How do we get these points across without sounding like we're lecturing?" Being a parent isn't *always* difficult, but when it comes to helping kids get through the rough spots in life in some sort of balanced way, being a parent is *very* difficult. Because there is some basic information that *anyone* needs in order to face this "serious stuff," we'd like to begin with that.

How Shame and Fear Come into Play

As you read through this chapter, it is essential to keep in mind the joint roles of *fear* (anxiety, worry, nervousness, terror, etc.) and *shame* (embarrassment, feeling broken or defective or bad, feeling better or worse than everyone else is) in the resolution of serious stuff. We knew a man in our profession who had a serious addiction to alcohol for many years, but as you might imagine it was very hard for him to admit this problem. He told himself that he had everything under control, that he was a therapist and therefore he couldn't be seriously addicted, that it was just the stress of his insufferable boss or his marriage or of trying to provide for his family that caused him to drink excessively at times. What he wasn't able to acknowledge for many years was that beneath all of those intellectual reasons lurked an immense pool of shame held in a container of terror.

The embarrassment was that somehow he *was* defective— that he was broken and therefore different from all the other therapists around him. The irrational part of him whispered from his depths: "If you acknowledge this problem, you'll be the laughingstock of the therapeutic community. You'll be a failure. Washed up. Nada." The second part, the terror, was that his wife, children, friends and colleagues would abandon him: "You won't just be the laughingstock, you'll be alone. They won't want to have anything to do with you. They'll ask you to move out, to live by yourself, in a hut, in the North Woods, until you die of hunger or hypothermia." There was also the fear of imagined punishment: "They'll take my license away. They'll prosecute me for practicing as an impaired therapist. They won't let me visit my children because I'm unfit."

Now, you may be reading this and saying to yourself, "That's pretty far-fetched. I know several adults who have faced serious problems like that, and I doubt that they ever *felt* those things." You'd be wrong. The *primitive parts of our unconscious selves* are not rational. They aren't logical. When fear and shame are left to escalate uncontrollably, the unconscious does an impressive number on us. When you read of terrible tragedies like suicides or homicides within a family, you can be pretty certain that those primitive parts took over first, and were then followed by tragedy.

Here's the kind of internal dialogue that can lead to either growth or tragedy:

> *I've got a secret* —> *I feel fear and shame about it* —> *I tell myself there's no one I can talk to about this* —> *I decide to manage it on my own* —> *I choose to hide* —> *whenever the topic comes up, I feel embarrassed, change the subject, get quiet, etc.* —> *the more I hide, the deeper it gets imbedded in my psyche* —> *I keep hiding* —> *the discomfort increases* —> *I reach a decision point and I either* —>

(a) talk with someone about it

or

(b) do something I'll really regret

The paradox of being a healthy human being is that *the very thing we are most afraid of doing is often the one thing that will make our lives better beyond measure.* This was termed the "neurotic paradox" by neo-Freudian personality theorists. When we are choosing to be healthy, we (1) *talk out* and (2) *work out* our problems, and when we are being unhealthy, we (3) *act out* our problems. Another angle on this is that whatever we continue to deny, we begin to act out. Admitting problems to ourselves and then sharing them with another person are very powerful steps toward taking charge of our lives.

Where the "Serious Stuff" Comes From

Our first book, *Adult Children: The Secrets of Dysfunctional Families,* was released in 1988 and is still selling regularly, in part, we believe, because in it we tried to clearly explain how and why a family system malfunctions, and what happens when it does. Current research on treatment outcomes show that people who participate in their own treatment improve more and faster than those who do not participate in their treatment. To participate, you need to be knowledgeable about the dynamics of your problem. With this in mind, we thought it would be helpful to quickly summarize the major things that psychologists and physicians look for when they're trying to help someone figure out what's bothering them.

As with everything in the realm of human behavior, there are biological causes for behavior. These include what you inherited from your parents, what happened to you when you were developing in the womb, and any biological factors that affected you after you were born. For example, you might have inherited a very calm temperament, had an uneventful time while in your mother's womb, a normal childhood, and then as an adolescent you might be exposed to some toxic chemicals that make you very hyperactive and tense. It would be up to you and your physician and psychologist to figure out where the tenseness is coming from, which isn't always as easy as you might think.

Has your good friend always been sort of grumpy and down on life, or is it worse now than it used to be? Is it because he's entered adolescence with all of the rapid changes going on, or is there more grumpiness there than you'd expect from just being an adolescent? Is he using alcohol or drugs? Has he changed his diet? Is he secretly taking steroids? Does he have a growth on his thyroid gland? Is there something wrong with his blood-sugar level? There are so many biological possibilities to explore and rule out that just when you think you've got it all nailed down tight, you have to start looking at the nonbiological factors that might be bothering him, which we'll look at in detail later in this chapter.

The Biology of the Brain

We find it especially helpful to our clients to zero in specifically on the biology of the brain. Over the years, we have had countless examples of new clients who had been treated with medications for depression or something else at one time or another, but had no clue as to how their brain chemistry was involved or what the medication might be doing. In our experience, informing people about these things helps a lot. When questions of brain biology apply to them, our clients get the following information from us or from the psychiatrist to whom we refer them. To our knowledge, no one has ever been *un*able to grasp this information, regardless of his age or education.

Neuropsychologists, physiological psychologists, psychobiologists, you name it—all tell us that knowledge of the brain is increasing so rapidly that it is very difficult for them to keep up. Nevertheless, there are some basics that are important for anyone to know if she or a loved one ever suspects they have a biologically-caused problem such as depression.

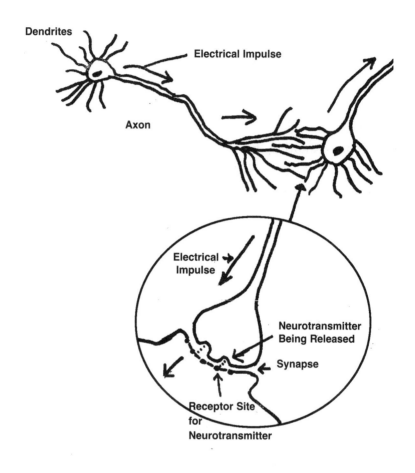

Neurons, the Synapse and Neurotransmitters

The basic unit of the nervous system is the nerve cell (neuron), which has the function of carrying messages (electrochemical impulses) around the body. When you raise your hand to scratch your head, the whole thing from start to finish is orchestrated by neurons. An electrical impulse travels down the long arm (axon) of the neuron and must then get across the space (synapse or synaptic gap) to the short fibers (dendrites) of the next neuron. The electrical impulse gets across the gap when a chemical (neurotransmitter) is released, passes across the gap, and locks onto receptor sites on the dendrites. This makes the membranes of the dendrites more permeable, allowing a flow of positive and negative ions, which sets up an electrical charge that travels down the axon of that neuron to the next neuron. Neurons fire according to an "all-or-none" principle—i.e., a nerve either has enough dopamine or serotonin or whatever on it to fire, or it doesn't. There's no partial firing. There is no rheostat, no dimmer switch on the nerves. Our clients find that piece of information very useful as they try to understand how and why the medication they're taking is or is not working.

If you have enough dopamine or serotonin or norepinephrine or whatever (there are scores and scores of different neurotransmitters in the human body—endorphins are another class of them) on the dendrites, then an electrical impulse is begun, and the nerve fires. If you have *almost* enough, but not quite, the nerve won't fire at all. If you aren't quite producing enough of one of these neurotransmitters, that part of your brain will be "depressed," that is, there will be a lessening of electrical activity in that part of your brain. *That* is all there is to it. To put it another way, a person who is clinically depressed because of a short supply of a certain neurotransmitter is no different than a person who isn't producing enough insulin and therefore has diabetes, or a person who isn't producing enough enzymes to digest milk and so gets gas when he eats ice cream.

It is therefore quite ill informed for people to refer to depression as some sort of unique or bizarre craziness instead of as a shortage of a certain chemical. The kind of depression described above is a *physical problem,* nothing more, nothing less. Every human being has at least one notable physical problem, if not several. If you or the people around you have the mistaken belief that there are perfect human specimens out there, we encourage you to go earn a college degree at a respectable university, making sure that you get a broad education that includes courses in biology, psychology and related fields. You may find yourself embarrassed to discover how limited your understanding was. The *norm* is for humans to have physical flaws, and it is the many physical flaws that each human has that make us so unique and so interesting.

There are, of course, other physical problems that can affect behavior adversely. There can be serious effects surrounding problems with growth hormone. People who have a true diagnosis of attention deficit hyperactivity disorder (ADHD) have been shown to have some identifiable differences in brain structure or function. Then there are all of the children whose mothers drank alcohol or ingested other substances or medications that affected their fetal development, resulting in behavioral problems later on. With all these possibilities, if you or someone you care about seems to be struggling with something that may have a biological cause, we hope that you or they choose to get the physical work-up that will lead to the proper diagnosis and treatment.

Family Causes

Let's go back to your friend who has been grumpier than usual. What are some *non*biological factors that could be contributing to his nasty moods? Are his parents fighting a lot? Does his mother share her personal problems with him? Is his father gone so much that he sometimes feels like he has no father at all? Are his parents controlling and critical? Are they lax and permissive? Is he scared that he isn't doing as well in school as everyone expects of him? Any and all of the above can easily cause someone to become angry, even rageful.

Families are incredibly complex, which makes them fascinating to learn about, work with and be a part of. It is especially fascinating that most of what goes on in any family is *covert,* hidden, under the table, unconscious. Because it is so complex to be part of a family and because we have so many different things to do and learn every day as we try to live our lives, the majority of what goes on *has to be* below the conscious level. Our brains would short-circuit if it weren't mostly unconscious. When someone respectfully and constructively criticizes you, do you immediately get defensive ("Yeah. Well *you* did it worse the other day!" or "I did not!")? If so, do you *consciously* choose to get defensive, or do you just do it *automatically?* Some people automatically reply to constructive criticism with something nondefensive like, "Oh. I didn't realize I did that. I'm very sorry if I hurt your feelings."

Augustus Napier and Carl Whitaker wrote a book about the experience of family therapy, giving it the intriguing title of *The Family Crucible,* which is exactly what a family is—a crucible. Inside of this container are all the rules for living that we are going to learn before we leave home. Below are some of the *categories* of those rules and patterns.

1. Perfectionism—Remember the extremes. Expecting competence is good. Expecting perfection makes everyone miserable, disappointed, and either angry or depressed.

2. Rigid Beliefs and Rule Systems—Religion is good. Rigid religion, or anything else, is not good. The tree that bends with the wind endures. The tree that remains rigid breaks.

3. The "No Talk" Rule—Uncomfortable topics are left alone, only to burrow deeper and deeper into the depths of the family where they eventually undermine everything, and often result in the fragmentation or even destruction of the family. Secrets can have a powerful effect on family members.

4. Inability to Identify or Express Feelings—See chapter 4.

5. Triangulation—Mom asks you how your brother is doing. Dad talks to you about his problems with Mom. Your sister tells you to go tell Dad something. Triangles in families make people feel connected, but it's always in an icky way.

6. Double Binds—You're damned if you do and damned if you don't. I tell you to clean up the garage. You start cleaning up the garage. I yell into the garage to interrogate you about whether you finished your

homework or not. Do you rush up and do your home-work, only to be yelled at for not cleaning the garage?

7. Enmeshment—Everyone's business is everyone else's business. Mom is sad, so you are sad. Dad wrings his hands and frets and worries until you get home, on time, as you said you would. He doesn't *say* he's wor-ried, but you can feel it. Your Dad screams at your brother, and you feel guilty. Everyone is tangled up in everyone else's lives. Rather than caring for each other and assuming that each of you is okay, you smother each other with what looks like love, but is actually not.

8. Physical Abuse and Neglect—Slapping, kicking, hit-ting, beating, starving, forcing to eat food, not get-ting you proper medical or dental care, not providing adequate clothes or shelter, allowing or encouraging the use of drugs or alcohol, and overworking, among others, are all forms of physical abuse and neglect.

9. Emotional Abuse and Neglect—Excessive guilting; blam-ing, shaming, name-calling, put-downs, comparisons, raging, belittling, teasing, making fun of, laughing at, nagging, verbal assault, endless lecturing, overpro-tecting, smothering, babying, denying your reality ("you don't feel that way"), failure to set limits or pro-vide structure, not listening to or hearing what you say, never going to any of your school activities, not taking an interest in what you're learning, not being around much due to work or other activities, and let-ting you run your own show are all forms of emotional abuse and neglect.

10. Sexual Abuse and Neglect—It is estimated that 28

percent of all girls and 17 percent of all boys will suffer *physical* sexual abuse at least once before they reach the age of twenty-one at the hands of someone who is at least five years older than them. Roughly half of this abuse happens in their own home, and someone they know perpetrates much of it. Then there are all of the *nonphysical* forms of sexual abuse and neglect, like inappropriate nudity, making a sexual joke or sexual innuendo out of everything, being prudish about sex, seeing sex as dirty or evil, or leering at you or others.

11. Vicarious Abuse—When your dad beats up your brother, you suffer, too. You suffer the immediate distress of seeing the violence being done to your brother, and then you suffer the delayed distress of wondering if it will happen to you next. If it never happens to you, you also suffer "survivor's guilt," like the survivors of the Holocaust who wondered why they had been spared, and who felt so badly about the others who died.

There is no such thing as a perfect family. All families have strengths and shortages. The goal of self-discovery is not to demonize your parents and siblings—it is to understand how you tick and then to change the things you want to change about yourself, and be grateful for the ones you simply want to keep as is.

People Do Get Help: Depression

It is common for people to wait until they are in the middle of a crisis before they ask for help. Many people operate this way. There are a few fortunate people who have learned to seek advice or assistance before the crisis point has been reached. Either way, it is usually wiser to yell for help before you "go down for the third time" than it is to drown.

Over one in five Americans can expect to get some form of depression in their lifetime. Over one in twenty Americans have a depressive disorder every year. Depression is one of the most common and most serious mental health problems facing people today. Even the majority of adults who come to us for therapy do not have a very clear idea of what depression looks like or of its causes, despite their often high level of professional education. The symptoms of depression are not just feeling sad and blue, they also include being irritable and angry, tired or agitated, indecisive, feeling like a "loser," feeling "stuck," eating too much or too little, sleeping too much or too little, and losing interest in normally enjoyable activities. In fact, we administer the Minnesota Multiphasic Personality Inventory (MMPI-II) to each person with whom we work because the test usually picks up depression whether we catch it right away or not. At times, depression can be well hidden.

Depression can be caused by a number of things. First, there are biological causes, which include a genetic, inherited predisposition to have a shortage of certain neurotransmitters that send signals from one nerve cell to the next, as we described earlier. You can also become depressed if what you do or say never matters. As psychologist Martin Seligman discovered, we can actually *learn to be helpless,* and learned helplessness often leads to depression. Some people were taught to be "too nice," which translates into the belief that any anger at all is bad. We know that anger is a good, healthy emotion if expressed well. The belief that "a good boy or girl never gets angry" is a double bind because *all* people get angry at times. This impossible belief system often causes us to hold our anger in and even turn it against ourselves, sort of like the body rejecting its own tissue, which results in depression. Depression can even be caused by the way people in the family *think.* If you think that everyone is out to get you, that the world is basically a bad place, that nothing you do will ever matter, that you will never be able to get what you want or need in life, then it would make sense that you might get depressed.

Here is how one teenager came to deal with his depression. William had been displaying many of the symptoms of depression for a couple of months, and his parents finally asked him how he was doing. They were agonizing over how to approach it because some of the same symptoms crop up when a person is struggling with chemical dependency, with learning difficulties at school or simply with normal adjustments to being a teenager in high school. They finally decided to just casually ask him how he was.

"So, how are things going, William?"

"Uh . . . okay, I guess."

"You seem to be struggling with something."

"Huh? Why do you say that?"

"You've seemed sort of distracted, sort of distant lately."

"Oh. I've just been busy with school. I've had a lot of homework."

"Oh," they continued. "Well, just remember that we're here if you ever need to talk about anything."

"Okay," he replied as he headed up to his room to call some friends.

That was pretty much it for awhile, but the seed had been planted. William's parents had let him know two things: (1) that they noticed him and cared about him, and (2) that they were available, but weren't going to press him on it for the time being. William felt his problems close around him a little tighter at the same time that they seemed to get bigger and less manageable. He hadn't realized how negative he was becoming, until a group of his friends responded to a comment he made by chiming in, "It's William. The voice of doom." A few days later, William made a negative comment in class in response to a discussion on the environment. ("I don't think anybody *does* care what happens to this planet.") William noticed that his teacher paused for just a split second before going on with the discussion, and that the look in her eyes in response to his comment was concerned and/or puzzled. He felt embarrassed, almost exposed, but not quite. He realized he was having a hard time concealing whatever it was that was gnawing at him.

He was over at his best friend's house one evening, and finally mustered up enough courage to talk a little bit about how he was feeling. "Frank, do you ever get down about things? You always seem to be so 'up.'" He half expected Frank to either laugh, look shocked, or run out of the room, but Frank hesitated nervously and then answered him.

"Yeah, sometimes. My parents were pushing me hard about school last year, and I was down quite a bit."

"I hadn't noticed."

"I hid it pretty well. I figured I could figure it out on my own."

"Did you?"

"Not exactly. I finally went to Mr. Peterson and talked to him about it. That helped a lot, actually."

"I never knew that. What's Mr. Peterson like?"

"He's a good guy, actually. He listened. He didn't lecture me. He asked me what I thought would help. I don't know. It just felt good to talk to an adult about it."

"Did it help?"

"Yeah, I think so. I got some ideas about how to deal with my parents better, and just knowing that I had somewhere to go with this, besides to my parents, made a big difference. I mean, I love my parents, but they were part of the problem. I didn't know how to talk to them about it." They were both silent for a moment, and then Frank asked, "Why do you ask?"

William swallowed hard and said, "Oh, I've been wondering . . . I . . . uh . . . have I seemed really negative to you lately?" He looked nervously toward Frank, watching for that imagined reaction again, but again it didn't come.

"Actually, you have been kind of negative lately. It hasn't bothered me, but I sort of wondered what was going on. I felt kind of bad when everyone teased you the other day, about being the voice of doom."

"Yeah. I hate it." William was sitting at Frank's desk, and now he began to play the video game that was silently waiting on the screen. "Maybe I'll go talk to Mr. Peterson."

"Can't hurt. He's a good guy."

William wasn't about to go marching right into the school counselor's office the next day. He was way too afraid and ashamed. He made several passes by the office, almost like strafing runs by an F-18 jet fighter, except that the only things he fired were nervous glances at Mr. Peterson's closed office door. Four-and-a-half weeks after his brief conversation with Frank, William opened the door and walked in to the tiny waiting area in Mr. Peterson's office. Mr. Peterson came out with another student a few minutes later, and William made an appointment to see him the next day.

It was almost like he'd jumped across the Grand Canyon. He was so relieved. At the dinner table that night, William casually mentioned that he had made an appointment to see Mr. Peterson "to work on some school stuff." His parents said they were glad that he'd made that decision, and without overdoing it, they added that it sometimes takes guts to ask for help, and that it's what competent people do. William felt better already.

He met with Mr. Peterson on several occasions, and then Mr. Peterson said that he thought William was showing some of the signs of clinical depression, and that he'd like William to think about going to see a psychologist outside of school for an evaluation. William mustered up some more courage, and then talked to his parents about it. They were relieved, and said that William should go ahead and set up an appointment, and that if he needed any help handling that, they'd be glad to pitch in. William made the call and then went to his first appointment. At the end of it, the psychologist said that he had all the signs of depression, and that he'd like William to consider going to a psychiatrist for a medication evaluation. The psychologist also took plenty of time to explain to William how neurotransmitters work, and how antidepressants work, so that William would know what the psychiatrist was doing and why.

The psychiatrist agreed that William was depressed, and said that he wanted to try an antidepressant for awhile to see if it might help. William was reluctant at first, but then realized that it was a trial run, not a lifetime commitment, so he agreed to try it. He also set up another appointment to talk with the psychologist about some of the nonbiological things that might be contributing to his depression, like how bad he felt at times that he might not be meeting his parents' expectations. The psychologist also suspected that he was mad about his parents pushing him, but he didn't say that right away.

Antidepressant medications like Prozac or Paxil are not addictive like the tranquilizers Xanax or Valium. In most of the cases that we've seen, the changes that people notice are subtle, and yet very significant at the same time. Some describe it as a veil being lifted off of their heads, or as being able to see things more clearly. Others describe it as a weight being lifted, or a dark cloud lifting. It is very common for people to say things like, "I still have the same everyday problems that I've always had, but when I walk out the door each morning, I don't feel like they are insurmountable anymore. They feel manageable. They aren't out of control, not so huge, not so looming."

It is also common for people to say things like, "I don't

want to cover up my problems with a drug," but that is a misunderstanding. An antidepressant is not like alcohol and marijuana, which *do* cover up our problems so we don't deal with them. Antidepressants don't *keep us* from dealing with our problems. To the contrary, they *allow us to deal with our problems* by reducing the feelings of paralysis that accompany depression. That is probably why the best treatment for depression that the research literature suggests is a combination of medication and psychotherapy.

That, in the end, is what William did. He and Frank were talking about it briefly several months later, and William mused, "It's amazing how much my life has changed since I first mentioned it to you. Am I ever glad. It wasn't good."

Frank replied matter-of-factly, "I'm glad, too. You seem a lot happier."

9

Find an Identity:
From Accepting Without Question
to Discovering Your Own Path

In general, indivuals who, between the ages of
fifteen and seventeen, never constructed systems
in which their life plans formed part of a vast dream
of reform or who, at first contact with the material
world, sacrificed their chimeric ideals to
new adult interests, are not the most productive . . .
(the adolescent's) passions and his megalomania are
thus real preparations for personal creativity.

—Jean Piaget, *The Mental Development of the Child*, 1940

I Am a Teenager, and This Is Who I Am

1. I am the girl next door to you who always smiles and says "hello" as I head off to school. I worry that nice people like you would be shocked if you knew what was going on inside of me. I am a nice person, too, but sometimes I think things or do things that I believe you wouldn't approve of.

2. I am seventeen. When I am out in the world on my own, I want to help heal people who are sick. My father died from cancer when I was thirteen. I miss having him watch my baseball games.

3. I am fourteen, and I am getting straight As in school. I want to help inner-city kids learn how to start their own businesses.

4. I drink almost every day. I love how I feel when I'm drunk. It takes away all my anxiety. Somewhere deep inside of me, I want to succeed like all of those kids I say I hate. I wonder if I can.

5. My father says to my little brother, "Frank keeps his room so well organized and neat. Why can't you be more like him?" I *hate it* when Dad does that. Jeff doesn't have to be just like me. If only Dad knew how much I admire Jeff because he loves to read. *I* read to get grades, not because I like to read. I feel like a fake.

6. I love to think and wonder. Sometimes while I'm driving, I wonder what the world would be like if we could produce enough food to totally wipe out starvation. It's so complex, though. There are so many aspects of the problem to keep in mind all at the same time.

7. My parents are driving me crazy. They have all these rules and chores and requirements and regulations. I just wish they'd stop nagging me. I know I have to do *some* things, but do I have to do *all of that?*

8. I don't fit in.

9. I'm great. I'm strong. I'm tough. Everybody likes me. Nobody knows me.

10. I cut myself with razor blades and knives and paper clips. I can't stop.

11. I'm going to get out of here as soon as I'm legally old enough to go. It's crazy here.

12. I love my job after school. It makes me feel important and useful and grown-up, even though I don't really need the money.

13. I like my life. I like school, my friends and my family.

14. I feel guilty that I have all the stuff I have. There's a voice inside telling me that I'm going to have to face some pain somewhere along the line if I ever want to grow up, but I'm so comfortable the way it is right now, too comfortable.

15. I'm more grown-up than a lot of the kids at school. I'm more serious. Sometimes they seem so superficial; their lives seem so trivial.

16. I had an epiphany when I reached high school because I realized that if I were going to make something of myself, I would have to start working hard. So I started to take my classes seriously. Some people thought I was weird, but mostly it didn't matter. They were too caught up in their own lives to be too concerned with me.

Why the Search Must Begin

Some parents understand what a teenager is supposed to be doing with her life. Some parents have a hard time understanding. Many are somewhere in between. What a teenager is supposed to be doing is nothing less than the monumental task of defining core parts of herself. Many of these parts will last a lifetime, while other parts will last for at least the next decade or so. What gets so confusing is that if she doesn't carefully examine much of what she learned from her parents, she won't get into adulthood.

It all begins with who we are when we're "little." It finishes up when we've jumped over enough hurdles to truly be "big." The hurdles are the key. Erik Erikson devoted most of his life to looking at these hurdles, and in the process he coined the famous term, *identity crisis.* The identity crisis is one of many stages that all human beings must go through before they can move on to the next square on the board. Following the identity crisis, we face a struggle for intimacy, then one of giving something back after all we've taken, and then one of putting all of it together before we die. Prior to this identity crisis, we face the struggles to find trust and hope, to be separate but still connected, to make things happen and to be competent.

There is a handful of people who revolutionized our understanding of human development in the twentieth century. Sigmund Freud is one. Jean Piaget is another. By building on the work of Freud and then moving well beyond it, Erik Erikson has probably done more to help us understand our emotional and personality development than anyone has in the past hundred years. Freud more or less said that our development centered on sex and death. Erikson said it was much more about how we all fit together as a society:

> *Personality can be said to develop according to steps prede-termined in the human organism's readiness to be driven toward, to be aware of, and to interact with a widening social radius, beginning with a dim image of a mother and ending with an image of mankind.*

What a fantastic way of looking at it, and how timely it is still. We start out as tiny little beings, totally dependent and unable to distinguish ourselves from our parents. A baby nurses at her mother's breast and doesn't have a clue that she is separate from her mother. She is hungry, she cries and the milk appears. It's all *her* as far as she knows. Then one day she cries and thinks about milk, but it doesn't appear. Mom is busy. "Wait just a darned minute! When I fantasized milk before, it appeared. I thought my fantasies were the same as reality—I thought that all I had to do was *want* something and it would appear! Bummer. But wait," the baby says, "I can handle this. I can wait a few seconds. Wait a minute! I can do this! I can wait!" Suddenly she real-izes that she is separate from her mother—that there are two distinct beings in the house. "What a rush!"

This ability to wait evolves gradually into one of the most important emotional skills that humans possess: the *ability to delay gratification*. Along with it develops the part of us that can deal with reality on a daily basis: *the ego*. Without this part, a human being is similar to a wild animal that acts and reacts on its primitive needs and impulses. There's a lot that's happening to us as we grow, even in the first few months of life. Erikson's contribution to psychology was to systematically describe what leads up to the identity crisis, and what follows it. In other words, what follows in the rest of this chapter is a road map to adulthood.

As you read through these passages, try to keep in mind that each stage builds on the strengths acquired during the previous ones, *and* each new stage includes the challenges of the previous ones, but in a different form. For example, the struggle for autonomy at age two is seen in the exciting statement, "no," which is a celebration of that two-year-old's emerging separateness. At age seventeen, this same need for autonomy shows up as "I'm going to go bungee jumping" or "I want to go to Mexico this summer as a volunteer." Because it also *depends on* the earlier stages being properly fulfilled, it also means that "I can only do these things well if I know that no matter what happens, you'll be there for me when I come back." Wise parents know this, and fortunate teenagers feel this unequivocally from their families.

Trust versus Mistrust—Birth to Eighteen Months

If I get my needs met pretty well, if I'm fed and diapered and held and talked to and played with and have safety and structure and enough predictability, and I'm allowed to form bonds with people—to attach—then by the time I'm a year and a half old, I should have a fairly good sense of trust that the world will be an okay place. If I am not taken care of consistently, if there is a lot of tension in the air at home, if I am screamed at or, worse, hit, or if I am left alone a lot, not played with, not held or snuggled, then I will learn that the world is unsafe, and my sense of trust and hope will be very damaged.

Towards the end of this first stage, if I am also allowed to be frustrated just a little bit from time to time, like the baby in the paragraph above, then my sense of trust will be even stronger because it will be a realistic trust rather than a Pollyannish one. After all, if I was given everything I wanted every time I imagined myself needing or wanting something, then when I grew up I'd be a rather unhappy camper. I'd be bitter, angry and disappointed all the time because life doesn't work that way. Can you imagine a grown woman stamping her foot and demanding that she get what she wants when she wants it—right now!—or else? Can you imagine what we'd call that woman? We might call her a prison inmate.

From the above discussion, you can probably see that this whole matter of learning trust is a bit tricky. We have to get what we need, but part of what we need is to not always get what we want. Didn't the Rolling Stones write some lyrics to that effect?

A wonderful mother we know was describing her eighteen-month-old son's first experiences at day care. She wondered if she was handling it properly by dropping him off, giving him a big hug, telling him she'd be back in two hours, and then cheerfully walking to her car even though she felt pretty guilty as he expressed his distress. She said that some of the other mothers kept going back, over and over, to reassure their kids. She noticed that the more the other mothers went back, the worse their kids' protests became. She thought that being clear and upbeat was a better way to handle it, but wanted to know what we thought. We told her we thought she was right on.

We also knew that she was a warm and loving mother who consistently met the needs of her little son, which is why she was able to report a few weeks later that her son was having a wonderful time at his brief visits to day care each week. She said, "Raising a child is such a challenge. You have to try to go right down the middle on these issues most of the time. Too much or too little, and it causes problems." When we work with adults who grew up in less-than-healthy childhoods, the first thing we address is trust because it's the first thing we all address right after we're born.

Autonomy versus Shame and Doubt—Eighteen Months to Three Years

These are not the "terrible twos." These are the "terrific twos." At around two years, kids and parents, with each other's help, figure out that someday they'll both mutually drop the lifeline that connects them. It won't happen in the near future, but now is the first glimmer of awareness that this is what it's all about. "Autonomy" means that you can stand on your own, even when others are asking you to stand with them. When everyone else seems to be in a frenzy of anxiety-driven hate, an autonomous person can say, "I don't want to deprive this man of his civil rights just because he's from Ethiopia or Alabama or Beijing or Ecuador or Iraq or Nebraska." An autonomous person can say, "I have a vague hunch that the universe is actually folded over and around itself somehow, and I'm going to pursue that hunch to see if there's any truth to it, even if everyone else thinks I'm a fool." An autonomous person can say, "Why don't you stop making fun of Susan? She's a lot more interesting than all of you are letting yourselves see."

The fascinating thing about how Erikson put this all together is that to be truly autonomous, we have to be pretty sure that we can depend on our home base, so to speak. In other words, *to be autonomous we have to be dependent.* Think about that one for awhile. It's one of the most crucial paradoxes in all of human experience. Powerful people weave it into the fabric of their lives. Powerful people need others, value others, respect others and care for others. They rely on the wisdom of others and share their wisdom with others. They lean on others when life gets too big for them and let others lean on them. They trust that no matter how bad things become, life will still be ultimately kind to them if only they learn to surrender.

People who haven't yet become powerful feel that they don't need others. They become angry if you suggest that they might need others, and try to take care of others as a way of "buying" relationships. They can't become more competent because they fear learning the wisdom of others. They let others lean on them, but don't lean on others. They believe that no matter how good things are now, things will go to hell before you know it. The exciting thing about all of this is that becoming truly powerful is something that anyone can learn, any time, right up until the moment they die. It's a choice. When people make the choice to become powerful in this way, it is truly miraculous, and yet, like all things of the greatest importance, it is quite ordinary. From interacting with, loving, and being loved by their family and friends, powerful people learn that the most important aspects of life are the ones that are the most ordinary.

If autonomy isn't acquired early on, the resulting stance toward life is one of shame, embarrassment and self-doubt. If parents stop a little child when he tries to become a separate person, either by saying "no" or by toddling off into a corner of a safe, fenced-in yard to look at the flowers, he starts to believe that his *will* is bad. His will tells him to go out into the world to discover it, and in doing so to discover himself. Wise parents want him to do this, but they stay safely nearby to ensure that he doesn't do something life-threatening like running into the street and getting hit by a car. Overly fearful parents don't want him to venture out into the world much at all because their anxiety is too big, so they confuse those times when a child needs to be on his own with those times when a parent should intervene.

The resulting shame and doubt go like this: *I try to go out into the world, occasionally, apart from my parents,* or, *I try to think in ways that are different from my parents. When I do, the people upon whom I still depend for life tell me that I can't—that my will is bad. So I give in and feel like I am bad. I give up. I am a good boy, but I have no will. I feel incapable. Other kids go out into life and discover what is out there, but I don't. I don't know why. The only time I feel okay is when I am attached like glue to my parents, but I don't feel okay there, either. I am so confused.* Or:

I rebel, exerting my will no matter what, but without guidance and clear limits, I exert my will in ways that make others not want to be around me. This makes me feel shame and doubt out in the world, too. I am trapped. No matter where I try to move, I am doing it wrong.

Can you see what a bind that is? That bind could easily be untangled, if only his parents could loosen up their grip *just a little bit.* That's the key, by the way. If his parents stopped caring altogether, he'd still be stuck with all that shame again because no one would be guiding him. It's just loosening up the grip a little bit that's needed. Then he can feel guided and protected while he still feels like he can exert his will in the world and discover things. *That's* what this stage is all about. Good, healthy, strong parents aren't afraid of their kids becoming mad at them for setting good, healthy limits. Good, healthy, strong parents aren't afraid of seeing their kids discover things, either.

Initiative versus Guilt—Three to Six Years

Initiative means making things happen. It means stepping outside of ourselves, like sharing a secret with a trusted person or auditioning for a part in a play. It means "to initiate something," to start something. When you go into the garage and start sawing a two-by-four in half, you're taking the initiative, whether you're ten or a hundred. When you apply for a job or for enrollment in a university, you're taking the initiative. When you ask someone out for a date, join an organization or volunteer for an assignment in class, you're taking the initiative. When you audition for a play and your family tells you that you were foolish to do so, you'll feel guilt and shame—that you did something wrong, and that you're stupid.

When you start sawing on that two-by-four and someone tells you that you have no business trying to learn how to cut wood, you feel like you're doing something wrong, even though you're doing something very right. When you apply for a university in another city and your family tells you that they'll be crushed if you attend a university in another city, you feel bad—guilt and shame. Guilt is sometimes very good, like when you think of hitting someone and stop because you'd feel guilty if you did. Guilt is good when it causes us to develop a healthy conscience. Without healthy guilt, you'd be a sociopath. But when you feel guilty for taking the initiative in positive ways, then the guilt is paralyzing.

Parents help their children progress through this stage in the same way they help them progress through the previous one—i.e., by creating a fairly wide chute for their kids to go down, with plenty of room for them to initiate new things, but safe enough walls to keep them from doing something destructive to themselves or others. Parents help by taking the initiative themselves, too. If you see Mom or Dad pick up the telephone and call to find out where the best stores would be to buy camping equipment, when you need something and aren't sure how to locate it, you'll be much more likely to ask someone, too. If you hear Dad and Mom complain a lot about never having the right camping equipment, and about not knowing where to find any, but that's all you ever hear them do, then, of course, you'll learn how *not* to take the initiative.

The Nike Corporation has permanently glorified taking the initiative with their slogan "Just Do It!" If you think about it for a few moments, you'll see the connection between being able to "Just Do It" and having the prerequuisite trust and autonomy. For a boy to walk up to a girl and ask for a date requires trusting that life will turn out okay even if he doesn't always get what he wants. If we know we have others upon whom we can depend, then sticking our necks out in such a risky way doesn't seem impossible. If we have sufficient autonomy rather than paralyzing shame, we'll feel like we can stand alone now and then, which is exactly what you're doing when you ask someone out for a date.

Now, imagine that you've asked someone out for a date, and this person is someone you've *really* wanted to ask out for a long time—you have very strong feelings for this person. Imagine that this person graciously declines your offer, saying gently that she is already going out with someone else. Next, imagine that you're pretty down about this. Noticing how dejected you look, your parents ask what's the matter, and you tell them. If your parents listen well, rather than passing judgment or giving advice, and are supportive, then you'll feel better. You'll feel loved and supported, which will lessen the sting of the rejection. You'll be much more likely to ask another person out in the future. Imagine what you'd feel like if your parents don't care, don't ask or don't notice how you're feeling. Worse, imagine that when you told them, they criticized you for thinking anyone would want to go out with you in the first place, or they were hurt and dejected themselves because they can't bear to see their child grow up. When it comes to taking the initiative, can you begin to see how important the ability to depend on our families is?

When we work with adults who have problems taking the initiative, they often discover that they are either paralyzed by a lot of unhealthy guilt (as opposed to healthy guilt), or that they had so many things done for them when they were growing up that they simply never learned how to make things happen. That's why one of our seven worst things that good parents do is "baby their children," i.e., infantilize their kids by doing too much for them, all with the good intention of making childhood less painful than their own childhoods had been. The unhealthy guilt that many people feel can sometimes be described as feeling sorry for or pitying someone. Unfortunately, these feelings are often based on the belief that most people are very fragile, breakable and delicate, which simply isn't the case. This is particularly difficult for individuals stuck in cruel relationships to understand. They know they should leave, but they're so afraid of hurting the cruel people's feelings that they keep staying. The irony is that people who are cruel to us hardly ever worry about *our* feelings. Sometimes we have to "Just Do It!"

Competence versus Inferiority—Approximately Six to Eighteen Years

Competence comes from learning those skills required to survive in your particular culture. If you were living several thousand years ago, these skills might have included how to build a shelter out of trees or stones, how to track wild animals, how to build a fire and how to make a spear tip. Today, these skills include how to communicate in written and verbal forms, how to use a computer and how to use mathematics. No matter when the era, human competence has always and will always include social and political skills—i.e., how to get along with other human beings while getting your needs met, too.

As we discussed at length in chapter 4, self-esteem comes from becoming competent and from having people in our lives who are crazy about us. Because everyone has different genetic gifts, it certainly isn't necessary to become competent at everything. All that's required of us is that we learn the basic skills needed to make it in our current culture, and then at least one specific skill that we can eventually use to make a living. These specific skills include how to be a machinist, a carpenter or cabinetmaker, a hairdresser, a physicist, a doctor, a teacher, a hunting guide or anything else.

The emotional competencies that we need include: how to get along with others, how to ask for what we need or want, how to be part of a group, how to lead, how to follow and take direction where appropriate. These are all minor, however, when compared to the two-part centerpiece of emotional intelligence: how to *delay gratification* (wait for things) and how to *empathize* with our fellow human beings (how to recognize feelings from others' nonverbal signals, how to use one's own experiences to help understand how others might be feeling, etc.). The inability to wait for things, and the related inability to tolerate frustration, are at the heart of most of the damage that we cause each other, from domestic violence, to robbery and murder.

From about age six on, we are supposed to be acquiring all of these wonderful skills at home and at school. For some kids, this poses a problem because more of these skills should be learned at home than at school. Over the past fifteen years or so, many parents have gotten so overextended themselves that they have tried to transfer to teachers more and more of their parental responsibilities. Teachers simply don't have the time to be parents in the classroom because their job is *to teach*. If this is the situation in which you find yourself, you may need to ask for more of your parents' time and attention. If they still don't seem to be able to give you what you need in these areas, then you'll have to learn them elsewhere.

Learning social and political skills, and emotional intelligence in general, can be done outside of the home. It is important in this case to be sure not to get into a "blind leading the blind" situation, which many of us do. If we have been repeatedly let down by our parents, it will be hard for us to try to lean on other adults. It'll feel a lot safer to find other kids upon whom to lean. In many cases like this, what we learn won't necessarily be wrong as much as it will be incomplete. For example, part of empathy is to put yourself in the other person's shoes. So, if a friend is getting in over her head with alcohol or drugs, you might identify with her embarrassment and fear about the prospects of being "found out" and having to get help. In this case, you might keep encouraging her to try to handle her problem "on her own." At the same time, you will keep covering for her behavior in various situations. If you had a little deeper empathy, based perhaps on your own direct experience of having to face a problem like this head on, you might handle it a bit differently. You'd still be friends with her and you'd still be supportive, but you probably wouldn't do things like cover for her, and you might not encourage her to handle it on her own, because you'd know firsthand that this doesn't work very well.

In order to get into adulthood with as many of these social and political competencies as possible, nothing helps more than having guidance, support, and direction from trusted adults. Finding those adults may be difficult if they don't exist at home, but it's worth continuous effort until you find them. We guarantee it.

Identity versus Identity Confusion—Thirteen to Twenty-Five Years or So

We have thought about this age range for many years. Erikson originally estimated this period to be between twelve and eighteen. The reason this span is so long in our estimation is due to extended education as well as extended dependency on the family. In any event, if a child has developed enough trust, autonomy, initiative and competence, then she is ready to tackle "the big one"—the search for who she's going to be.

The "accepting without question" part of this chapter's title refers to the fact that when we're little and so much more dependent on our family for survival, we pretty much accept as gospel what our parents give us. The earth is round? It doesn't *look* round from here, but okay, I'll buy it. Judaism, or Catholicism, or Buddhism, or Taoism or Protestantism is the one true religion? Okay, I'll buy it. Most people can't be trusted? Most people can be trusted? Okay. Republicans or Democrats or Independents are demons? Okay. We like to go to the ocean, or the mountains, or the desert, or Europe, or Mexico, or Canada for vacation? Got it. We believe that being gay is a sin? We believe that being gay is a biological variation? Whatever.

As Jean Piaget discovered and systematized in his theory of cognitive development, as kids enter adolescence, many of them also begin to enter a new phase of thinking called *formal operations.* At the same time that we begin to discover who we will be as adults, we also gain this new way of thinking, which helps the identity search in some phenomenal ways. With formal operations, we are able to hypothesize, think systematically, empathize more deeply and more accurately, and think abstractly instead of so concretely. It makes sense that this would be the time when we start to question and wonder. The ability to question and wonder, by the way, is the greatest compliment to creation that we can imagine. When you get right down to it, our ability to think beyond where we are right now, and our drive to know and understand, are what make human beings so marvelous.

All of a sudden our parents turn around and in place of that snotty two-year-old who said, "No, I can get it myself," they hear a fourteen-year-old say, "Dad, I'm not sure that all Republicans or Democrats or Independents are demons." Of course, as with the two-year-old, there are two ways to respond to this newfound willfulness and autonomy. One response is to be shocked and saddened, followed by vigorously attempting to control the child's behavior completely. The other response is to be pleasantly surprised and excited. This is followed by very clear, deliberate, gentle and thoughtful efforts to provide enough structure—to define the widely separated walls of that chute—so that the child or adolescent has plenty of room to maneuver, but not so much room as to get hit by a car, literally or figuratively.

The search for identity ultimately answers the question: Who am I? As such, it includes what you will be most interested in while in school, what you will believe in, how you will eventually make a living, what lifestyle you will have, who your friends will be, and what you value. This search is just that: a search. A search means you have some hunches about where to look, but you don't know exactly where. In this case, it also means that while you have some hunches about what you're looking for, you don't know that exactly, either. As Erikson taught us, there are three basic states that a person can be in during this identity crisis:

1. *Moratorium*—This is the searching phase. Kids need to question and wonder, and try on different hats. It helps to take school seriously and to do things like internships and volunteer work. It helps to have summer jobs that give you various life experiences. It is especially helpful to have teachers who love to teach and who make you work hard, and who know you can learn, because then you will. It helps to have parents

who value struggle, and who aren't afraid of your growing up and being different from them.

2. *Foreclosed*—This is where people end up if they don't go through a searching phase. They very often look like they have a good, clear, adult identity, but they never seem to question or wonder or try on different hats. This solution to the identity crisis seems like such a good one on the surface, especially for parents and children who have anxiety about growing up. Often, teachers, parents and clergy who see kids stuck in this foreclosed state are actually relieved because being in this state means that their children will never question anything. When you think about it a little more, however, not having enough life experiences before settling on an identity is a pretty scary thought. After all, before you choose a marital partner or a career, it's probably a good idea to date a number of people and to try a number of different jobs.

3. *Confused*—If we don't have the previous stages filled in pretty well, and if we don't have adequate support and resources as we go through adolescence, the negative outcome that Erikson called identity confused or diffused happens. An adolescent or adult who is in this place may look like he's searching, but in fact he's floundering. The *flitting* from one job to the next, from one major in college to the next, from one relationship to the next, lacks the *direction and struggle* of the moratorium state. Beneath it is intense anxiety, too, whereas beneath the moratorium state is an anxiety that is energizing rather than paralyzing. A

person who is identity confused needs a steady, stable, structured world, and a parent or mentor or therapist who is steady, stable, structured and reliable, in order to find an identity.

Have a Dream

Martin Luther King Jr. immortalized the call to have a dream. As quoted at the beginning of this chapter, Jean Piaget gave his blessing to adolescent idealism. Our dreams come out of our personal experiences, which are unique and valuable regardless of what anyone tells you. Many doctors grew up with a parent who had a chronic illness and vowed then and there to do something to alleviate the suffering of others. In his earlier films such as *Poltergeist* and *E.T.,* Steven Spielberg was acclaimed for making the lifestyle in the middle-class suburban tract house, like the one he grew up in, an accepted setting for movies. By doing so, he formalized the suburbs as one of several legitimate features of our society and culture. Even more personal were the ghostly terrors in *Poltergeist*—the tree branch outside his window that eventually crashed through the window and tried to attack him, for example—that were from his own childhood fears and nightmares. A psychologist might say that he was gaining mastery over those experiences by weaving them into his films.

When he began to work on *Schindler's List,* his Academy-Award–winning black-and-white masterpiece about the Holocaust, people first of all wondered if he would be able to pull it off. Then there was the usual musing about his working through his own issues of being Jewish in a world that still looks askance at Jews. If you look carefully and systematically at his films, you will see a wonderful progression of themes and increasing maturity that is nothing less than the process of identity development shared with the entire world. He was creating from his own experience all the way along, until one day he completed *Schindler's List*. We can only surmise what that must have been like for him—how transforming, deepening and healing for him.

In chapter 2, we took note of psychologist Martin Seligman and his work on learned helplessness. Dr. Seligman is past president of the American Psychological Association and perhaps one of the finest individuals this country has ever produced. When he was thirteen years old, his father was stricken by three strokes at the age of forty-nine, which left him "permanently paralyzed and at the mercy of bouts of sadness and, bizarrely, euphoria. He was physically and emotionally helpless."[22] Seligman went on to write that, "This was my introduction to the suffering that helplessness engenders. Seeing my father in this state, as I did again and again until his death years later, set the direction of my quest. His desperation fueled my vigor."[23] Seligman has devoted the lion's share of his life to the study of learned helplessness and learned optimism, and as we have said before, he is the one who says that *successful people fail, they just don't quit.*

The search for an identity is like mustering up enough courage and faith to jump across a crevasse in the pitch black of night, hoping that it is only three feet deep, rather than three thousand. The searching is hard, it's painful and it's exhilarating. It scares our parents at times, and it scares us at times. Then, after a few years of *systematic searching,* you'll wake up one day and realize that you've *embraced your life for all it's worth*—as your own.

10

Start Learning to Stake Out the Extremes: It's *the* Universal Skill

Our senses can grasp nothing that is extreme . . .
too far or too near prevents us seeing; too long
or too short is beyond understanding;
too much truth stuns us.

—Blaise Pascal, *Pensées,* 1670

The Universal Skill

Picture a needle gauge that, rather than being round, is straight, linear. It has gradations on it, and at one end it says "Never," and at the other end, it says "Always." In the middle area, which takes up about a third of the gauge, it says "Sometimes." The needle can travel freely back and forth between the two extremes. Our job as evolving human beings is to try to keep the needle in the fairly wide middle area as much as possible, always mindful that perfection is not an option. The goal is to do as good a job of it as we can based on where we're starting, remembering that if we could always do it perfectly, we wouldn't be human beings.

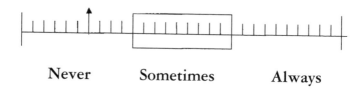

Never   **Sometimes**   **Always**

Just about everyone who has ever worked with us as a client of any kind knows how much importance we put on the skill of *staking out the extremes*. Whether they be parents wanting advice on how to be better parents, individuals trying to overcome unhappiness, court-ordered clients who have problems controlling their tempers, recovering alcoholics or addicts, corporate executives wondering how to do a better job managing their employees, or teachers and psychotherapists wanting to know how to be more effective in their work, we always end up coming back around to the importance of staking out the extremes. What we have discovered is that the more severe or intense the problem, the more valuable it is to do this.

We call the ability to stake out the extremes *the universal skill* because it is unquestionably and pervasively useful at all ages and across all cultures and belief systems. There are few circumstances where this ability to locate the ends of a continuum, and then the middle range in between, is not of the utmost utility. There are many times when it is life-saving. You may have noticed our use of the extremes and the middle range throughout the previous chapters of this book. Now, we want to focus on it directly.

Setting the Stakes in the Ground

The first thing that we do ourselves when trying to sort something out, or that we ask our clients to do when there is confusion about what is "right" or "healthy," is to (1) draw a line across a piece of paper and then create a scale using the line:

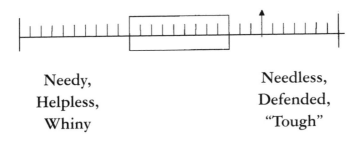

Needy,	Needless,
Helpless,	Defended,
Whiny	"Tough"

Then we ask them to (2) give a few examples of these because people sometimes understand things in the abstract, but have a hard time translating that into concrete, real-life terms. We might ask, "How would I know if someone were being needy, helpless and whiny?" You might answer with, "I had a friend last year who couldn't make any decisions for himself, and when things didn't go his way, he complained and groaned and moaned about it to anyone who'd listen to him. He'd ask for help with things he should have been able to do at his age, like writing a check or filling out an application form. He was a real pain."

We might then ask, "And what would it look like if someone were 'needless'?" One teenager replied with, "My uncle is like that. He not only won't ever ask for directions, but he won't ask for help doing his taxes, fixing his car or operating his computer. The poor guy spent two entire weekends trying to untangle a software mess on his computer, by himself. Then on Monday afternoon while he was at work, his sixteen-year-old son finally called tech support at Compaq and had it figured out in thirty-five minutes! What a waste." The same teenager gave another example as he described his mother. She was a woman who "lets everyone lean on her for emotional support and advice—people are calling her at all hours of the day and night—but she swears she doesn't have anyone she can lean on when things are tough for her. She does, but she just won't let herself be vulnerable with anyone."

Fill in the Middle

Then we ask people to try filling in the middle. A client might say, "Hmmmm. The middle. Well, it would be like someone who is open and available to others, you know, lets his defenses down sometimes, and yet one who is self-reliant and independent. He would ask for help when he needed it, without sounding helpless and inept. He would be able and willing to help others, but not all the time. Not night and day. He would put some reasonable limits on how much he took from others and on how much he gave to others. Let's see. What else? He'd be capable of getting emotionally close to others, and he could tolerate and enjoy others being close to him. He'd probably be seen as strong but warm and open."

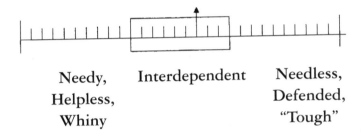

Needy, Helpless, Whiny	Interdependent	Needless, Defended, "Tough"

At this point we might jot down the word "interdependent" and then tell our client that he's done a very good job of defining the extreme ends of this continuum, and of mapping the middle ground as well. As people do this exercise over and over again, they report that subtle changes begin to take place inside of them. For example, when a friend says something insensitive to you, you may feel the sting but may not blow it out of proportion. For example, "When Bob said he thought I was stupid for going out with Kathy, I felt really bad. I didn't like what he said, but I guess we can continue to be friends for now, *and* I'm very glad that I went out with Kathy." When people become conversant with the extremes and the middle between them, they find their reactions to things are more balanced. They find themselves less troubled by life's challenges, and they find that they hurt themselves and others less often.

When you look at everything in black-and-white, either-or terms, it can certainly make for an exciting news story. It can create a lot of drama and hype. People often feel energized when operating in the extremes. Of course, if you assume that the average American isn't bright enough to grasp the subtlety and richness of life, then looking at everything in the extremes is the way to go. While some people believe that having a balanced, moderate response to life is boring, it's actually a far cry from boring. In fact, when we think of extreme responses, a few of the images that come to mind include "crude," "unrefined," "lacking subtlety," "using a sledgehammer to pound in a nail," "embarrassing," "lacking finesse," "tactless," "unrefined," "artless" and "dull."

Imagine how much effort and struggle it takes a person to learn enough about art, music or astrophysics in order to have the deepest appreciation possible for a painting, a symphony or an event a million light years out in the universe. You might rightfully argue that one needs no education in order to appreciate these things, which is why we appended the modifier "deepest" in the sentence above. Remember, too, that education includes "education of the senses," as in learning to discern and appreciate the differences between fine coffees or the fragrances of tropical flowers. It is one thing to pick up a two-hour-old, dried-out McDonald's hamburger at the drive-through and then scarf it down as you race down the freeway. It is another thing to sit down at a sidewalk café in Paris and enjoy a leisurely lunch that was prepared with care and presented with artistry, as your afternoon fills up with warm conversation and companionship.

As many Parisians will tell you (if you are displaying even a modicum of restraint), not all Americans are ugly.

Variety Is the Spice of Life

Because it is so important to be able to discern the boundaries of the extremes and the location of the middle ground, we will continue with several more examples. We encourage you to struggle with these, and to come up with specific examples of your own. The more cases to which you can apply this principle, the better. Variety is, indeed, the spice of life when it comes to this skill.

Permissive, Lax Parenting versus Strict, Rigid Parenting

You might not be surprised to learn that the majority of teenagers we know tell us that as much as they hate to admit it, they appreciate having parents who are able to be parents. Adults who grew up with no responsibilities, no rules and no expectations have a very hard time making it in the world. Everything feels unfair and too hard, which means they are essentially crippled. Teenagers who have parents who let them do anything they want tell us that it feels like a disguised form of neglect, and we agree.

On the other side of the coin, adults who grew up with strict, rigid parents are really hard on themselves and on those around them, and they often have a difficult time finding out who they really want to be "when they grow up." Finding any success or joy in life is also difficult.

Teenagers need to have *some* consistent rules and responsibilities, and then they need a lot of room to explore and investigate life's options.

Silently Rageful, Pouting, Passive-Aggressive Silences versus Openly Rageful, Violent and Destructive

We've covered this in the chapter on feelings, but it's worth a second look. Anger is a healthy, positive emotion that is there to help us protect ourselves and also make constructive changes. When it is clear, direct, appropriate to the occasion and *under control* (whether loud or soft), then it is usually helpful. When it is out of control (whether loud or soft), it is damaging. Pouting, ignoring, not speaking to someone for days to punish them, and rolling your eyes and making faces are all forms of rage and/or disgust and contempt, and, as such, are very destructive.

It is a source either of some humor or some anguish in many households to hear parents talking about their teenager's eye rolling and sighing. It is important for you to know that whether or not your parents are passive ragers, are active ragers, or express healthy anger, it is your job to learn how to do the latter by the time you get into adulthood. The consequences of not doing so are just too great.

Lax or Nonexistent Religious or Spiritual Training versus Rigid, Strict Religious or Spiritual Training

Religious or spiritual organizations are supposed to help you celebrate your beliefs within a community, which should bring you together with others and keep you together. Religion is supposed to help you rise above your human limitations. It's supposed to bring out the best in you. Many people are baffled and disgusted by the amount of violence and hatred that is perpetrated in the name of religion, and rightfully so. For example, many people we know who call themselves Christians are embarrassed by the awful things that human beings do to each other in Jesus' name. Jesus preached tolerance, forgiveness, understanding, inclusion and love of one another over picayune rules. He would likely be crucified even faster were he alive today.

Whether your family professes to be Jewish, Christian, Muslim, Hindu, Buddhist, agnostic, atheist or some sort of New Age amalgam of all of the above, we have found it valuable for people to find some balance when it comes to their beliefs. This is especially true in how they practice those beliefs and in how they pass those beliefs on to their children. It is often useful to pose the following question to yourself every once in awhile just to stay on the up-and-up. How would the God that I believe in judge the following two people: a person who struggled her entire life with never being sure if there was a God or not, but who treated others with love, respect, kindness and justice, and a person who professed and actively participated in an organized religion, but treated others dishonestly, cruelly and with little compassion?

Helping Others Too Much versus Caring for No One but Yourself

Finding the middle ground on this continuum is one of life's most rewarding and challenging ongoing struggles. If you help everyone else to the exclusion of yourself, you will be bled dry. You will eventually be unable to do anything for anyone, including yourself. If you stray too far in the other direction, you will become narcissistic, hollow and very alone, even if you have managed to surround yourself with others who admire the shell you have created around your inner self. A simple example of these extremes would be someone who hardly ever buys anything for herself and a person who only buys things for herself.

People who are able to stay in the middle much of the time are compassionate without being maudlin. They have encountered and endured many of life's painful struggles with grace and dignity. They do not value babying others, nor do they value being unkind and cruel. If you drove away from the house of someone like this while you were intoxicated, they would call the police and pray that you be arrested before you kill yourself or someone else. Their heart would go out to you in your embarrassment and anger, and, if it were appropriate, they would be there to help you through the ensuing crisis. This mix of realism and empathy is the closest manifestation of true love that we can think of. It is, we suspect, what lets the Mother Teresas of the world, including those right in your own neighborhood or homes, do what they do.

Taking Few Risks versus Taking Excessive Risks

Much of what we take for granted in our daily lives was achieved or understood at great risk. Thousands of years ago someone got into some sort of vessel and began to travel across the open seas. He may have died trying, but that first attempt simply spurred others on, and eventually . . . well, the rest is literally history. When philosopher-scientists first proposed that the *sun* was the center of things rather than the earth, the proposition was so disturbing to contemporary people, including leaders of the church, that it rocked their very foundations and resulted in the ostracism or even execution of those who supported this new theory.

Change is one of the few constants in the universe, but it is also one of the scariest. When developmental psychologist Jean Piaget defined intelligence as the ability of the organism to adapt to its environment, he was saying that change is a constant, and that our job as intelligent creatures is to adapt to those changes. The weather in California is so uniformly kind that we forget that California occasionally has floods, unpredictable freezes that destroy crops and, of course, earthquakes. Just when we think we have everything under control, life proves us wrong. Life is therefore always interesting, either because of what it isn't doing, but could be doing, or because of what it's currently doing.

Without risk, we would still be dying of Black Death. We would still believe that we were the absolute center of the universe rather than a tiny planet sitting towards the edge of the Milky Way, a humble galaxy among millions, all of which are hurtling out toward the edges of the universe itself. People who are still terrified of risk and truth do not even want to believe *that,* which is unfortunate because the humility that it affords us is the foundation for our deepest spirituality.

Knowing when to take risks is as important as knowing when to not take them. Teenagers are notorious for taking risks. If we take that as a given, then the question becomes, "Will you try to push that needle into the middle now and then? If you try, will you find people, hopefully your parents, but if not your parents then someone else, and if not someone else then just life itself, who will stop you from straying too far?" If you can push that needle into the middle, by the time you are thirty or so you will most certainly be healthy, happy, and perhaps even prosperous in a way that is meaningful to you. Remember that never taking risks can be just as serious as taking too many or too extreme risks. Not to risk is not to be alive. You can die of an accident in your own home, even though you hardly ever leave home for fear of having an accident.

Compulsive Cleaning or Neatness versus Being a Terrible Slob

Are all teenagers' rooms capable of being declared disaster areas? Not all. Are they all condemnable by the Board of Health? Some are. Do you have to don hazardous-materials gear before entering a teenager's room? Not usually. Are some teenagers compulsively neat and orderly? Yes. Can it be a serious problem to be a terrible slob? Of course it can. If you are so completely disorganized that your room *always* looks like a disaster area, you may have trouble finding your homework, let alone completing it. You may be wearing clothes that are so filthy that not only do people not want to be around you, you could actually develop serious hygiene problems. You should also think about living with someone else when you leave home. It could get pretty stressful.

Being a compulsive cleaner or "neatnik" has its advantages, but it also has its problems. If someone is truly compulsive, they may have a diagnosable emotional disorder that includes a lot of anxiety about any lack of order whatsoever, or an irrational fear of dirt and germs. If you aren't severe enough to be diagnosed with obsessive-compulsive disorder (OCD), you may be severe enough to be making others' lives and your own life miserable. Remember to try to keep the needle in the center of the gauge as much as possible. Order and cleanliness are good and necessary, as long as attaining them doesn't take up so much of your time and energy that there's nothing left of you at the end of the day. Putting things other than order and cleanliness first is important at times, too, as long as doing so doesn't create an emotional or physical health hazard.

All Work, No Play versus Putting No Energy into Work

Americans are some of the hardest-working people on earth. As a consequence, Americans also have a lot of problems surrounding how much they work. American children also have some pretty serious consequences affecting them because of how much their parents work, or, in some cases, because of how many hours *they* work before and after school. In some families, work is so overvalued that all anyone does from dawn until late at night is work. Some people even refer to these as "human doings" instead of human beings. Whatever the label and whatever the reason, many people struggle with this one a lot.

In chapter 6, we mentioned that there was some sort of serious "disconnect" going on in American families, with the Littleton tragedy being just one tragic example. How could all of that have been happening under parents' noses without *someone* noticing or asking? Our answer was, and still is, that it couldn't have happened in families where people are emotionally connected. Dylan Klebold drove a BMW and lived in an upscale house, so everything must have been okay, right? As we've said for over two decades now, *wealthy isn't necessarily healthy.* Some videotapes were found that Klebold and Harris had made prior to their deaths. The following quote (with italics added by us) is from an *ABCNews.com* report on December 13, 1999:

> *In one videotape, the boys predict the very thoughts that would race through the minds of their* parents. *"If only we could have reached them sooner or found this tape,"* Klebold *imagined his parents would say. "If only we would have searched their room,"* Harris said. *"If only we would have asked the right questions." The two also talked about how easy it was to plot their attack without anybody noticing, with Klebold recalling* his mother once saw a gun handle

sticking out of his gym bag and assumed it was his BB gun. *In a haunting passage, Harris said they "came close" to being caught one day when* a gun-shop clerk called his house and told his father, who answered the phone, "Hey, your clips are in." But, according to *Time,* he said his father told the clerk he had not ordered any ammunition clips and did not ask whether it was a wrong number.[24]

We would have asked the gun-shop clerk who the clips were for, who ordered them and why they were ordered. Then we would have gone to our kids and gotten to the bottom of whatever it was. Members of the media, who all seem to be bright and well educated, have a strange habit of "going dumb" when something like this happens. Some even said that these families were "not dysfunctional." *That* is impossible, if Klebold's and Harris's quotes above are at all accurate. If accurate, they point to profound neglect.

While being disconnected, whether from overwork or any other reason, can have serious consequences, *not taking work seriously* can obviously have life-threatening consequences as well. While wealth doesn't insure health, having enough money to cover the necessities of life, with enough on the side for emergencies, is a huge stress reliever in and of itself. Kids who learn to enjoy work and to eventually take responsibility for their physical needs are acquiring habits that will serve them well for a lifetime. Kids who are not required to do chores or to have responsibilities are being set up for a lot of disappointment, misery and paralysis later in life. There are few things more pitiful or embarrassing than a full-grown adult who is still a baby inside—incapable of working, following through or caring for himself.

Crying All the Time versus Never Crying

Much of this was covered in the chapter on feelings, but we want to mention it again because so many people get so confused by it. When we shed tears of sadness rather than to wash dirt from our eyes, a chemical change takes place in the brain, and our blood chemistry changes. This was proven by Dr. Robert Frey at what used to be St. Paul Ramsey Medical Center.[25] We are literally healing when we cry. Something is being corrected or repaired. To never, or hardly ever, shed tears is a sign of emotional constipation, and constipation of any kind isn't good for you. Human beings are capable of crying for a reason. Sadness is "the healing feeling."

To be so sad and distraught that you are crying all the time and at the drop of a hat also indicates something is wrong. Life presents us with many reasons to be sad, which is why we are capable of crying, but that kind of extreme sadness can mean a number of things are wrong. You may be in the midst of one tragedy after another. You may perceive as tragedies those things that other people perceive as problems and challenges. Your brain chemistry may be out of balance, as might happen with some clinical depressions. You may actually be guilty or angry, but never learned how to manage those emotions. You may be enmeshed with and carry the emotions of some other family member, like a mom or a dad. Last, you may have never learned how to contain your emotions, so they spill out all over, out of control much of the time.

Always Following the Rules versus Hardly Ever Following Any of the Rules

Teenagers are notorious for breaking rules and testing limits, which is fine, up to a point. The push to achieve autonomy and eventual independence from the family requires some rebellion, as we have seen. However, research shows that teenagers who have problems with addiction, truancy or trouble with the law go on to become adults who have more adjustment problems than others—more divorce, more alcoholism, more job failures, more trouble with the law, etc. The conclusion you might want to draw from this is that there is an invisible line here that you don't want to cross. When the chips are down, it's what you've learned from your family about self-respect and respect of others, and how supported by your family you feel, that will determine whether or not you choose to go over that line.

This scale is very similar to the risk-taking scale above. Without some breaking of the rules, we'd all be living in the Dark Ages, or much worse; but if everyone broke the rules all the time, it would be worse than *Lord of the Flies.* Somewhere between these two extremes lies our form of government. The U.S. Constitution was written with two clear understandings: that human beings make mistakes and that times change—which is why it was written so that it could be amended. An example of how this works is when

Americans approved the prohibition of alcohol, realized that it was a social experiment that failed, and voted it out.

Sometimes it is even necessary for good people of sound mind to break the rules rather than wait for a Constitutional amendment. If an issue is serious enough, you may find yourself directly violating the law because of your moral convictions, which, by the way, happens a lot less often than we'd like to think. Harvard's Lawrence Kohlberg, who studied the moral reasoning of several key figures in the Free Speech Movement and Vietnam War protests of the 1960s, discovered that although their surface behaviors were often similar, they fell into two distinct categories. There were (1) those who were operating at a very high level of moral reasoning, and who, as a result, had reverence and respect for the very law-making system that they were protesting. They often graciously accepted the punishments they were given for breaking the rules. Then there were (2) those who were protesting out of revenge or vengefulness as a way of acting out rage at their parents via society and social institutions, and who were very narcissistic, self-serving, focused on media attention and unwilling to accept responsibility or consequences for their actions. This group was operating at the very lowest of Kohlberg's levels of moral reasoning.

People who always try to follow all the rules are in a trap of a different type. Years ago, this person might have been called a "goody-two-shoes." Whatever the label, compulsive adherence to rules can be very problematic. An extreme example would be what happened in Nazi Germany. In trying to comprehend how the Holocaust could possibly have happened, Stanley Milgram conducted a series of experiments after World War II that shook the psychological world. He discovered that the majority of college students he tested, regardless of how independent, enlightened, rebellious or humanistic they were, administered what they thought were excruciatingly painful shocks to fellow students in another room "because the experimenter, a college professor and psychologist, told them to do it, and that it was sanctioned by the university." [26]

Milgram was studying obedience to authority. What was so hard for everyone to admit was that bright, middle-class Americans were just as likely to cave in to pressure from authority figures as anyone else. The disbelief was so great that the study was repeated over and over with various populations, but the same results were always found. People would sit there and continue to push buttons that they thought were sending excruciating shocks to other human beings (actually, they were actors who were screaming in the next room) because an authority figure prodded them to continue. If you're sitting there reading this and saying to yourself, "But *I'd* never do anything that cruel or stupid," we ask you to think again. We guarantee you that, *given the right combination of circumstances,* most people would do things that they would later feel horrible about having done.

Never Daydreaming versus Always Daydreaming

Here it is again. If people didn't daydream, we'd still be back at the beginning of history. When you sit and gaze out the window, not hearing a word that is being spoken in your midst, your unconscious mind is working overtime. It's a form of play, in the sense that Piaget defined it, as your mind churns out images and fantasies and scenarios. People solve a lot of problems when they're in this dissociative state, so to never take the time to daydream can be a real shortcoming.

Daydreaming can also be a way of avoiding painful feelings or experiences. Kids who live in high-conflict homes, in alcoholic homes, or in homes where there is physical or sexual abuse tend to dissociate more, and daydreaming is one way to do it. Over the years, we have had a number of people who came in for help after a second or third automobile accident that was largely because they "zoned out" while driving. (We all zone out while driving from time to time, so just because you do that doesn't mean that you are dissociating excessively.)

Saving Compulsively versus Spending Compulsively

The key here is the word "compulsively." Saving is something a lot of Americans don't do enough of, while overspending is way too common in this country. Saving, whether it is money or other resources, is part of a thoughtful, planned life. Creating reserves of energy, money, time, you name it, is often a good thing to do. Saving like Scrooge in Dickens's *A Christmas Carol,* however, creates a stance that closes you off from life, and that, in his case at least, only visiting spirits could remedy. That sort of penny-pinching is usually driven by a disproportionate fear of the things over which we have no control—life being the most obvious one. In other words, this behavior often reflects a simple lack of faith, hope and trust.

Similarly, compulsive spending is considered in many circles to be an addiction that can devastate a family, and not just through the many bankruptcies that it causes. When people are damaged enough—and we all are damaged to some degree—they develop what Robert Bly called "a hole in our soul." An addiction is a way to try to fill up that hole. Some people temporarily drink away their loneliness or emptiness or fear. Others use food to soothe those painful feelings. Still others spend themselves into oblivion. As with any addiction, what begins as a good and fun thing quickly deteriorates into destruction.

To move the needle into the mid-range here means that we must be thoughtful without being stingy. We must be willing to sacrifice security at times for the sake of future payoffs (i.e., take calculated risks). Energy isn't just to be conserved; after all, what is the point of energy unless it is used now and then? Energy is to be conserved and used in a balanced, wise way.

Victim versus Perpetrator

When other people hurt us all the time, the cure is not to turn around and become the one who does the hurting, but that's what a lot of us do. The needle on the gauge floats effortlessly from one extreme to the other as Dad's boss screams at him, Dad screams at Mom, Mom screams at you and you scream at the dog. Letting others hurt us regularly is part of a syndrome that Freud called neurosis, and that later became known as codependency. Hurting other people a lot is called being an offender, a perpetrator or a bully.

The cure for these two extremes, as we have said before, is to acquire power that is tempered by grace, dignity, respect, and the acceptance and depth that can only come from experiencing and acknowledging the pain of loss.

In Closing

We would like to close this chapter with a quote that we have used in two of our earlier books because it conveys so elegantly how simple yet complex human beings are, and how important it is to transcend the polar opposites in life. It is from a book that we found is a favorite from high school literature class—John Steinbeck's *Cannery Row.*

> *Its inhabitants are, as the man once said, whores, pimps, gamblers, and sons of bitches, by which he meant everybody. Had the man looked through another peephole, he might have said saints and angels and martyrs and holy men, and he would have meant the same thing.*[27]

11

The Labrador and the Cockapoo

By perseverance the snail reached the ark.

—C. H. Spurgeon, Salt Cellars, 1889

Our story continues: They awoke the next morning and Abby picked up Sam very carefully. She was losing strength and she didn't want to make any mistakes when they were this close to their goal. A couple of hours later, they came to a clearing in the forest again, only this time what they saw were cars. They went a little further along the road, and then they saw buildings. As they approached one of the buildings, a woman came out and seemed to be walking toward them, so Abby quickly wheeled around and jumped behind some trees. She put down Sam, and they both peered around from the tree to see what the woman was doing. She was putting something into a container, and making a whistling noise. Suddenly a big German shepherd bolted from behind another building, raced over to the container, and began to eat. The woman patted him lovingly on the head, and he wagged his tail.

"Doesn't look too threatening to me, Sam."

"No. I think it's time we came in from the cold."

It was really as simple as that. They took a deep breath, and then walked out from behind the tree and toward the woman and the other dog. Sam was limping, but he had wanted to do this last stretch on his own. The dog finished the last bite of his food, looked up from his bowl, and wagged his tail as he saw them approach. The woman looked at Abby and Sam—one limping, both tattered, cold, haggard and hungry—and she nearly burst into tears. They could feel her warmth and compassion. They breathed more easily.

She approached them carefully in case they might be aggressive, and they wagged their tails as best they could. She knelt down and patted Abby on the head. Then she looked at Sam, and said, "Oh, you poor thing. Let me help you." With that, she lifted Sam up in her arms and tried to feel the bones in his front legs. Sam yelped in pain. "We need to get you to a doctor right away. Those legs need to be x-rayed," she said, solemnly, "but first I'll see if you two want some food and water." With that, she brought them right into her house, filled two bowls with water, and placed them on the floor. Sam and Abby took long, long drinks. Then she placed two bowls on the floor, inside of which was some kind of squishy meat, which they devoured in almost an instant.

Suddenly, they were overcome by exhaustion. Abby went

over to the corner of the room where there was a rug on the floor that was drenched in morning sunlight. She curled up in a ball and started to doze off. Sam hobbled over and curled up against her, with his head in the opposite direction and resting his head over her legs, and he dozed off, too. "Well," the woman said to the German shepherd, who had been patiently watching this whole drama unfold from a spot next to the woman, "I guess the vet can wait. Those two must have some story to tell." The German shepherd looked lovingly up into her eyes and wagged his tail. She smiled warmly, patted him on the head again, and said, "You're such a good boy."

Sam and Abby slept for most of the day. Around 4:00 P.M. they were alert enough for the woman to put them in her car and drive them to the vet, whose office, it turned out, was only five minutes away. There, Sam and Abby were both given a clean bill of health on their internal organs, with the vet saying he hadn't heard hearts and lungs that strong in his entire career. Sam's front legs were broken. The vet said they might heal okay without surgery, but because cockapoos were so accustomed to springing into the air to climb and jump, it would be better to set them surgically. He put Sam under, pinned the bones back together, and wrapped the legs firmly. The vet was soon amazed to see Sam awake from the anesthesia long before expected, and wagging his tail no less. "There is something exceptional about these two dogs," he said, shaking his head in amazement. "There is something very deep and grounded about them. Something spiritual."

The woman agreed. She knew just what she was going to

do with them, too. She knew of two people down in Minnesota who would be the perfect ones to care for these two. She brought Sam and Abby back to her house, where they curled up together, in that same way, and slept. She placed a call to the United States. A few days later, a car pulled into her yard and a man and a woman emerged. Sam and Abby ran up to greet them, wagging their tails. Sam darted away and, as male cockapoos are accustomed to doing, returned with one of his newly acquired toys in his mouth to show his guests. They looked at Sam and Abby, then at each other, then to the woman, and said, "These two dogs are astonishing."

It was as simple as that. The man and the woman loaded Sam and Abby into their car and began the leisurely drive down to Minnesota. When they arrived, the man and the woman brought Sam and Abby into their home and let them explore the new surroundings. The two dogs stood at attention when they went out onto the deck overlooking the backyard and the forest beyond. The smells of the oak trees and all of the animals living in the forest monopolized their senses. A small herd of deer was munching away on some leaves. Geese were honking overhead as they were preparing to fly south for the winter. Squirrels cavorted in the trees to the left, to the right and in front of them. There were squirrels everywhere. They could hear dogs barking everywhere, too. Sam whispered to Abby, "There are worse places on earth." Abby nodded peacefully.

They went back into the house and searched for the man, who turned out to be at his desk, typing on a laptop computer. Sam and Abby trotted quietly into the office and sat next to the man, who turned around for a few moments and petted both of them on the head very affectionately before finishing up his work. Abby looked at Sam and Sam looked at Abby, then they both looked at the computer screen again. Sam began, "What does that say on the screen? Something about pet supplies?"

"Yes, Sam. It's some sort of place to order food and supplies for animals. Here, if I stick my head up close to the screen . . . wait . . . there, I can rest my head on his arm and see perfectly."

The man looked down at the big yellow Labrador retriever head resting on his arm, felt the warmth of Abby's affection, and patted her on the head again, saying, "You're such a good girl, Abby." Abby could now read the screen perfectly. She just watched as the man typed away at the keyboard, entering commands that caused different pictures and words to appear on the screen. It went from pet supplies to political candidates to the late-breaking news, and then with a click of a button the screen went blank. The man got up and walked out into the living room.

"Sam, I think I know how to work this now," Abby said.

"But Abby, how can we make the keys work? We have paws, not fingers."

Abby came back, "I know. But there's always a way. Remember your dilemma back at Dead Dog's Gorge. There's always a way if you're willing to be flexible enough."

Suddenly Sam looked almost enchanted. "'Flexible enough.' That's the key! We need something that's flexible enough but also strong enough so that we can attach it to our paws somehow and then manipulate those keys on that keyboard!"

"Sam, that's brilliant!"

"Thank you, Miss Abby, but your unconscious mind was working overtime on this one. The key was that phrase, 'flexible enough.'"

"Do you really think the unconscious works that way?" Abby asked.

Sam replied, "Oh, not all the time, I suppose, but I think it works that way enough of the time that it's worth suggesting it as a hypothesis in a case like this."

"Well, Sam, you continue to be quite the gracious young alpha cockapoo. Giving me some of the credit for that brainstorm was very generous." Sam wagged his tail briefly and licked Miss Abby on the face. They found their way into the garage, where there resided all manner of tools, wires, copper tubing, canvas, old gloves and glue, among other things. No one knows exactly how they did it, but when they emerged several hours later, each of them carried an odd-looking pair of gloves. They were later to be mass-produced for all the dogs in Minnesota, where the literacy rate is perhaps the second highest in the world, next to Ireland. As you might have already guessed, they were canine computer keyboard gloves.

"Abby!"

"What!"

"I'm on! Hurry up! Get in here quick!" Sam had booted up the laptop computer and was already connected to the Internet.

"Sam, I saw him click on that symbol there . . . yes . . .

the one with the black Labrador with his paw up. What is that?" Abby asked.

"Lycos. Let's see what happens." Sam clicked the symbol, and up popped a screen with a blank box, in which he typed the word "Labrador." Then he pressed "Enter." Up popped a long list of Website URLs related to Labrador, including Labrador retrievers and the region of Labrador in Canada. Sam said, "Abby, I think we've found what we're supposed to do in our next life, here in Minnesota."

Abby queried, "What, Sam? Play on the Internet all day long?" She wagged the tip of her tail coyly, and then looked out the window with a disinterested gaze, intending to catch Sam off guard.

Sam almost barked, "Abby! You don't care about my idea? Abby! What's *wrong* with you this afternoon?" He was really rather perturbed at her sudden loss of interest.

Abby wagged the tip of her tail again, then jumped up on all fours and twirled around to face Sam, who was up in the chair, paws on the computer keyboard. "Sam! I think I'm following you. And it's a *great* idea!" Now Sam was taken aback. How did she know *exactly* what he meant? Maybe she didn't. Abby spoke again. "You're thinking we should get our own Web site, and then write about our lives back in the Far North, before we became domesticated. Then we should integrate the wisdom we acquired there with the newfound wisdom we acquire here, in civilization. Is that what you were thinking, Sam?"

Sam was dumbfounded, but thrilled. "Yes, Abby! That's *exactly* what I was thinking! Not only are you strong, grace-ful, compassionate and beautiful, you have a piercing, unmatched intuition." Abby would have blushed again, were Labradors wont to blush. "I think we should give this some serious thought."

"As do I, Sam. I think we could actually become authors, if we were willing to work as diligently at it as we have pursued everything else in life." Sam wagged his tail and licked her on the cheek again. They curled up together in the late afternoon sun and began to snooze.

When Abby awoke, she noticed that Sam was already awake. He had carefully taken some tissues out of the waste-basket in the office and had begun to shred them with his teeth, pushing them gently into a corner beneath the desk. "Sam!" she barked. "What are you doing?"

Sam replied very nonchalantly, "I am building a cockapoo nest. What does it look like I'm doing?"

"A cockapoo nest? What on earth is that?"

"It's what my breed sleeps in when we're in the wilderness," Sam explained. "We can't get outside where I could use leaves and moss, but I discovered that these tissues make perfect nesting materials. What do you think?"

"Sam, I think you're very resourceful."

"Do you think they'll mind?"

"Tissues shredded up in a pile under the desk?"

"Yes."

"I suspect they'll mind."

"But . . . ," Sam sputtered, "it's instinctive, like them caring for their young. I'm not sure I can help myself."

"You may not be able to. Can you limit it, though? You're so handsome. They may let you get away with it now and then if you don't get out of hand with it."

"I'll try. There. That nest is done, anyway. Now, where were we?"

"We were discussing our potential new life's work here," Abby said. Sam turned to look at her. "Sam, isn't it wonderful how the patterns in life are so fascinating? How closing one door often allows others to open? The trick to it all is that before the others can even begin to open, you have to risk closing the door, not knowing if others will ever open or not. It's like jumping off a cliff in the pitch black of night and not knowing whether it's a three-foot drop or a three-thousand-foot drop. Think of it."

Sam added, "I *am* thinking. I'm thinking of what would have happened if . . . well . . . you know . . . if we hadn't met."

"We wouldn't have gotten to where we are right now had we not made all the choices along the way that we eventually made," Abby observed.

"You do realize, Abby, that our faith is what got us through this. We could have given up anytime, but we didn't. We could have blown it right at the end. When we saw civilization for the first time, we could have let our fear dictate our actions, instead of our wisdom and faith. We could have hightailed it out of there and back into the wilderness . . ."

" . . . where you may or may not have survived," Abby solemnly noted.

"I might have. The vet said I might have. I heard him say that."

"That's true. You might have, or you might have spent the rest of your life getting more and more feeble and crippled by the day. Arthritis would have set in. It could have been pitiful."

"But we would have been in the wilderness, where we supposedly belong."

"Yes. There are always trade-offs in life, Sam. I guess it's all in what you do with the hand that you're dealt. Are you aware that every morning when you get up, you stretch like I do, with your front legs outstretched and your head down? Then, unlike me, you stand up and extend your left hind leg straight out, stretching it for an especially long time. Why do you do that?"

"I broke it when I was a puppy. It healed okay, but it's been a little stiff ever since."

"Did it stop you from jumping over Dead Dog's Gorge?"

"No, but it was stiffer than usual after that jump. Actually, it's a reminder of things—of my puppyhood, of what's important in life and what isn't, of how far I've come along life's path."

"So you don't regret it?"

"No. It's part of who I am now," Sam said peacefully.

"Well, this is who *we* are now, Sam. We live in Minnesota. We are domesticated. We have begun a most exciting new life that neither of us could ever have imagined just a few short months ago. Had we turned back into the woods that day, we may have made it, and that could have been okay, too."

"Yes, Abby. But this is going to be such an exceptional life. I can feel it in my bones."

"I believe you do, Sam. I believe you do."

"Abby, have you ever noticed that saying up on the wall

above the desk? The one over there, on the right side?"

"No. What does it say?" They both sat there, staring up at the saying on the wall, reading it silently to themselves, reflecting on the momentous changes in their lives. They each had a little tear forming in the corner of their eyes. It said:

> *Creatures usually fail when they are on the verge of success, so give as much care to the end as to the beginning, then there will be no failure.*
>
> —LAO TSU, *TAO TE CHING,* SIXTH CENTURY B.C.

Part III

Some Tips

12

Becoming Competent

The man who is afraid of asking
is ashamed of learning.

—Danish Proverb

A friend of ours described this scene recently: A twenty-three-year-old walked into his office for an employment interview. He was applying for a job as an entry-level computer programmer. Our friend began the interview by asking what training and experience the young man had. After giving an inappropriately brief answer, the young man added, "Have you ever thought of expanding your business to include an Internet-driven, automatic bill-paying service? My father is always complaining about paying bills. I'll bet that would be a great business. I have a lot of good ideas like that."

Our friend thought to himself, *Well, this young man is*

certainly taking the initiative here, but he gave a pretty weak answer to my question about experience and training, and he hasn't researched our business or the market very well. It's a good idea, but (1) there are already a lot of "dot.coms" out there for bill-paying, and (2) there's no way that idea would fit in with our business plan—we write custom software for small businesses. Well, I'll try to make the interview last a little longer so he doesn't feel quite so ashamed, then I'll get him out of here as gently and quickly as I can.

The *function* of what some call "adolescent rebellion," its very *purpose,* is to propel you out into the world—not so far that the tether between you and your family is severed, but far enough that you eventually become your own person. As you become your own person, you can generate your own ideas. Some of those will be new, if not for humanity, then at least for you. However, trying to generate new ideas without any foundation or competence regarding the ideas that came before you is pretty futile, if not downright grandiose.

We have worked with adults who tried to bypass this important step of building a foundation based on previous knowledge. They believed they had a better idea, and that they therefore didn't need to *learn* anything, they just needed to *teach* everybody their new ideas. After awhile, nobody listened to them because their ideas weren't very good. The purpose of learning what has gone before—things like history, math, science, art, poetry, how to repair an automobile engine, how to build a house, or how to interpret and understand great literature, is so that you (1) don't keep reinventing the wheel while thinking that you're creating something new and astounding, and so that you (2) have some wisdom, depth, perspective and connection to the rest of the human race as you leave home and go out into the world.

Adding to Your Competence Picture

There are all sorts of systems that you can use to assess your competencies, like grades, standardized tests, skill checklists and so forth. For some of you, those will be great; for others, they will be too formal—too much like school. One very helpful technique we have used is to keep a notepad and pen nearby (or a personal digital assistant [PDA] if you have one). When you catch yourself thinking "I wish I knew how to . . ." or "I'm secretly envious of her because she knows how to . . . ," then write it down. We find that most adults have something they wish they knew how to do. Many have had that wish for decades. The comforting thing about writing down these thoughts somewhere is that you then have a list of *desires* for skills or knowledge. In other words, you have *passion* inside because it comes from your soul, from your heart, from your gut, not from what someone else thinks you should be doing.

Many people actually *do* live lives of quiet desperation because someone along the line led them to believe that what they wanted to do wouldn't work or wasn't worthy. As we have pointed out in many of our writings, falling into this trap is an avoidable tragedy. If you draw a big circle on a large piece of flipchart or easel paper, and then label it "all the skills, vocations, interests and competencies that ever existed or *will* exist," then, of course, you'll have a container with an infinite capacity. If you take all of the billions of human genetic combinations possible and stir those in, you could double that, if it were possible to double infinity. When you're brainstorming your own potential interests and competencies, limiting the options up front isn't a good thing to do.

Find and Then Latch onto Someone Who Knows What You Want to Know

You can do some of this by reading about others, but at some point it is *almost* essential to find a living, breathing person to learn from. School is actually not such a bad place to do this if your dream requires skills or knowledge that a teacher or coach has, but it can be anyone, really. It could be a neighbor, a relative or, believe it or not, someone in your community that you've read about. You can call or write to let them know how much you admire what they've done, and how much you'd like to interview them about it. If you write such a letter, the chances are excellent that this person will give you at least one interview. Successful people, entrepreneurs and other self-directed, self-employed people like artists and writers, in particular, love to talk about their accomplishments, especially to a young person they can encourage and mentor. If you do one interview with this person, and it goes well, the chances of having more contact and even some mentoring increases.

That may sound corny, but it's not only what smart teenagers do, it's also what smart *people* do. For many teenagers and young adults, the critical juncture is that point when they decide that their desire to "do something with their lives" is greater than their fear of what their friends or family might say. Sometimes the even greater impediments are the fear and guilt that come with leaving their friends or family behind, figuratively, if not literally. It is a natural part of life to feel strong bonds to the group of friends with whom you go through school. It is also a natural part of life to leave home and friends "to seek your fortune" or "to see the world." Learning to grieve the loss of what was, and celebrate the possibility of what may be, is what being a successful teenager is all about. If you're willing to think about it with a slightly different twist, you may find yourself awakening to a new day in which you take your dreams, and yourself, seriously.

Here's a letter that a seventeen-year-old client of ours wrote to the CEO of a Minneapolis-based software-development company. Feel free to model your own letter after this one.

Dear Mr. Jornada:

When I read the article about you in the business section of the Minneapolis Tribune *this past weekend, I was so impressed with your software-development team and the way you have treated your employees that I had to write to you and tell you. I have been doing some programming on my own, mostly self-taught, and I realized that the work you are doing is exactly what I've been interested in.*

I am seventeen years old and a junior at Moundsview High School. I have gotten as much help, encouragement and support as I possibly can from my parents, a couple of friends, and one of my teachers. Now, I have an assignment to interview someone about his work, and although I realize that you are terribly busy, I would be honored if you would be willing to spend a few minutes with me for a brief interview. I have permission from school to do this any time during the workweek, at your convenience.

I thank you in advance for reading my letter, and hope that you will be able to meet with me.

Very truly yours,
William McIntyre

By the way, this wasn't his first letter, and it wasn't his first interview, but it's the one that eventually paid off. Every time he ran into a dead end, his father encouraged him to try again, telling him stories about his own disappointments and starts and stops on his career path. Whenever he felt discouraged and defeated, his father thoughtfully and without preaching helped him get back on track. This was the payoff. The interview led to a summer job that was nothing glamorous at all, but it landed him right in the center of a software-development firm. It didn't matter what he was doing there. He soaked it all in, and then came back for more the next summer, and the next. He began to write some code for a real project. He was assigned some more . . . and . . . well . . . the rest is history.

13

Mastering Feelings

W hen is man strong until he feels alone?

—Robert Browning, *Colombe's Birthday,* 1844

How Does Your Relationship Feel?

T he two lists below are reproduced here from our first two books. We still receive some pretty nice letters about them. They describe what it feels like to be in a healthy relationship and what it feels like to be in an unhealthy one. Many people have told us that these two lists have helped them evaluate whether to change a relationship, leave it or stay in it as is. Others have told us that merely looking at the two lists has helped them learn to identify their feelings better. Some people struggle with whether they really feel these feelings at all when it comes to their relationships.

Healthy Intimacy	Unhealthy Intimacy
whole	desperate
joyful	fearful
competent	anxious
interested	rejected
strong	angry
clear	confused
comfortable	abandoned
peaceful	exhausted
fulfilled	invisible
grateful	controlled
happy	used
excited	manipulated
trusting	empty
aloneness	loneliness
togetherness	identity-less

Rage Reminders

We use the following diagram regularly to help our clients who have anger or rage problems. They tell us that it is hard at first to make the connection between the "softer" feelings of fear, shame and hurt, and the "harder" feelings of anger and rage. They also tell us that once the connection is made, they have fewer problems with inappropriate anger.

R-A-G-E

Fear   Hurt   Shame

We'll pretty much give you a written guarantee that if you're feeling angry, a nanosecond before it you felt one of those other feelings. Did someone just make fun of you in front of a group of girls, and you'd like to throttle him? Why? Because you were embarrassed, humiliated, looked stupid, silly, foolish, felt like a geek—in other words, you felt shame. Did your mother just tell you that you couldn't go to your friend's party tonight because there won't be any adults there, and you're really mad at her? Why? You're mad at her because you're scared that your boyfriend might get interested in someone else if you're not there.

Feelings "Attacks"

Sometimes feelings can get so big that they feel like they're out of control. When this happens, it is *very* helpful to be able to label what is going on. You may have heard someone say that he had a "panic attack." A panic attack is fear (anxiety) that has moved up the scale far enough that it feels bigger than you *think* you can handle. Actually, you *can* handle it. If you pay attention to what's going on, you can become quite adept at handling it. Just imagine the scale we've talked about before, but now visualize it like a throttle on a jet airplane. When your anxiety moves into the high area, you want to take a deep breath and tell yourself, "It's just a panic attack. Nothing bad will happen." If you need to learn how to relax, by all means get a relaxation tape or do some biofeedback, and practice. Then it will be all that much easier to gradually pull the throttle back into the medium zone, at which point you'll notice the panic attack diminishing. Sometimes panic attacks can be so frequent or severe that they require medication in the beginning to help you manage them. Sometimes they're related to depression, and will diminish as you get help for that.

As you may have guessed, any feeling can be experienced as an "attack" in the sense we've just discussed. If you've ever shared some very personal things with people in a group, you my have noticed yourself having a "shame attack" after the group broke up and you were back outside and on your way home. You may have felt very exposed, as if everyone was watching you or talking about you, and you may have wanted to run away and never see those friends again. The same thing can happen if you flub a speech in front of everyone at school or if someone humiliates you in front of your classmates. It is normal to feel embarrassed in these situations. If you start to feel overwhelmed with shame, remember that it is just a "shame attack," and that you will survive it. Remember, too, that the quickest cure for a shame attack is to talk with someone—connect with someone—because shame is the feeling that we're different and don't belong. By talking with someone, it restores the sense of belonging and quickly brings the shame down into the medium or low range.

Emotional Flooding

Once emotional flooding has occurred in one or both partners, Gottman has shown that nothing but damage happens after that. He teaches people how to soothe themselves and each other, and how to postpone an argument or heated interaction as soon as flooding begins.

Emotional flooding is similar to having "feelings attacks." In chapter 5, we mentioned that University of Washington psychologist John Gottman can now predict with 94 percent accuracy whether or not a marriage will last. One of the most important predictors of a lasting relationship is how well you can *soothe your own* uncomfortable feelings. The other is how adept you are at helping to *soothe your partner's* feelings. When people are not very good at identifying feelings and are not very good at soothing feelings, the chances are huge that they will experience *emotional flooding* on a fairly regular basis. You are emotionally flooded when your feelings reach such intensity that you can't think straight, you want to flee the scene or you want to lash out and hurt the other person. You will have all the symptoms of physiological arousal, including rapid heart rate and elevated blood pressure, rapid breathing and muscle tension. You will also seem unable to soothe yourself. In other words, you are not on top of your emotions; they are on top of you.

In *The Soul of Adulthood,* we wrote that, "Many years ago we began to tell our clients that they would be well on their way to healthy adulthood when they could choose to be lonely rather than to hurt someone, to let someone hurt them, or to hurt themselves." One of your most significant tasks from adolescence through the mid-thirties is to learn how to do this. People who aren't able to do this are almost assured of doing destructive things to themselves and others in attempts to take care of uncomfortable feelings.

Feelings and Their Triggers

We thought it would be helpful if we gave a few more concrete examples of each of the basic feelings and some events that can trigger them. If you're ever confused about what you're feeling or why, reviewing this section might be helpful.

I become angry when . . . you snoop through my diary or
                                       my dresser drawers.

                                 you frighten me.

                                 you level a racial insult at anyone.

                                 you lie to me.

I am sad when . . .   a friend moves away.

                                 our vacation is over.

                                 I see someone suffering from
                                       poverty.

                                 I think I might have to end our
                                       relationship.

I am happy when . . .   you look up and say "hi" when I
                                       enter the room.

                                 I do well on a test.

                                 school is out for the summer.

                                 I spend time with you.

I am hurt when . . .   you make me the butt of your
                                       jokes.

                                 you criticize me.

                                 you cheat on me.

                                 you let me down.

I feel shame when . . .   I can't remember my lines
during the play.

my parents don't have time for
me.

you criticize me.

I realize I need to ask for
professional help.

I am scared when . . .   you storm out of the house, still
angry.

I think that I may not pass my
English class.

my brother, in the Army, is sent
off to war.

the fire alarm goes off upstairs.

I feel guilty when . . .   I let you down.

I steal money from my mother's
purse.

I rage at you and see the fear and
hurt in your eyes.

I try to make you do something
you don't want to.

I feel lonely when . . .   everyone is going out and I have
to stay home.

my parents don't have time for
me.

I believe one thing and my
friends believe another.

you end our relationship.

14

Breaking the Silence

Friendship, of itself a holy tie,
is made more sacred by adversity.

—John Dryden, *The Hind and the Panther*, III, 1687

Whom Do You Trust?

On a blank white sheet of 8½" x 11" paper, use a pencil to draw a big circle that fills most of the page. In the center of the large circle, draw a smaller circle one to two inches in diameter. Label that circle "me." There you are, smack dab in the middle of your social world, which at the moment is empty. The rest of the exercise is the hard part, and you may want to experiment with it a few times before you settle on a finished product. What you want to create is a map of your social world, using circles of differing sizes placed at varying distances from the center (you) to represent the strength and importance of the relationship *in your life right now.* This should be done *as it really is,* not as you wish it would be. In other words, you have to get really honest with yourself. That's what can make this difficult.

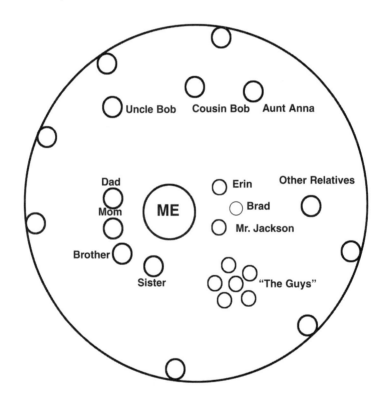

In the figure above, you can see one teenager's first attempt at doing this exercise for himself. Around and to the left of the circle labeled "Me," Greg has drawn four circles of equal size, representing his dad, his mom, his brother and his sister. To the right a little farther away, he has drawn a slightly smaller circle to represent his girlfriend, Erin. Next to her and just a tad smaller is his best friend, Brad. A little farther away are circles for the group of friends with whom he spends the most time. The next circles that Greg added were the ones on the outer edge of his social world. For some, the closest and then the most distant relationships are easier to plot out than the ones in the middle. So, on the outer edge, Greg has placed a number of people on the periphery of his life. These outer relationships, by the way, are very important in one's overall intimacy picture and should be carefully considered when doing this exercise. Sometimes people minimize these relationships "because they aren't very deep," but we caution against this. They *are* important.

At this point, Greg stopped and realized that his mind was beginning to go into high gear, with people's faces swirling around like a dynamic, free-flowing collage. "What about my relatives?" he thought. He noticed a slight tightening in his gut and an almost imperceptible increase in his breathing. "Is this anxiety?" he wondered. It was. When anyone other than a sociopath is called upon to do an exercise like this, there comes an inevitable moment when we are forced to admit that someone may not be as important to us as they "should" be. After all, a "nice" man should feel close to his sister. He "should" put her circle close to the middle of the map. Greg struggled with these relationships for quite a long time, until he finally began to enter them into his map. He winced as he put his Uncle Bob about seven-eighths of the way between the center and the outer edge of his circle. He was more comfortable putting his cousin Bob and his Aunt Anna there, too.

"Okay," he said, relieved. "The rest of my relatives can be represented by one circle." He drew one circle and labeled it "Other Relatives/Family." Then he had one more thought. "What about Mr. Jackson? I share more private things with him than almost anyone." He thought for a moment, and then put Mr. Jackson next to his family, but a little farther out.

The next steps are to sit back and reflect on your work, put it down and let it rest, reflect on it again, and make any alterations you'd like to make. Then look at each person, and ask yourself this question: If I were cutting myself, if I thought I was hopelessly addicted to marijuana, if I were seriously thinking about suicide, which of these people do I feel I could talk to about it? Keep looking at your diagram. Now, ask yourself this: If any of those things were going on with me *right now,* which person (people) *would* I talk to? That's the question of the day. When the chips are down, whom do you trust?

Be aware that when you do this exercise, you may wind up with a very different picture. When Sharon did hers, she discovered that she had several "empty accounts." In fact, her drawing contained only herself, her brother, her mother, and some classmates on the periphery. The difference between hers and Greg's is startling. The hopeful aspect of this exercise is that diagnosing the problem accurately and honestly is just the first step in the process. We have worked with hundreds of people with similar social maps and they have all made significant positive changes in their support systems. *Change is always possible. Change is a choice.* Sharon's next step was to admit these positive facts to herself, and to then begin systematically filling in the gaps in her social world.

Warts and All?

When it comes to emotional support, being around people who like and value you warts and all is often quite different than being around people who don't know about any of the warts, or who need to believe that there aren't any. At the same time, we find that it is crucial to discern the difference between those who love you unconditionally and those who put up with crummy behavior on your part. You may have heard the term "enabler" in various contexts. Providing no consequences for stupid or crazy behavior isn't really a sign of unconditional love. It's a sign that the person in question is so afraid of losing your friendship or love and/or is afraid that you are so fragile and weak that to react with a reasonable consequence for your inappropriate behavior is unthinkable.

For example, if you pretty much always tell your friends that you'll be somewhere at a certain time, and then pretty much hardly ever show up, we would hope that you eventually find yourself not included in people's plans. Your friends wouldn't be doing you any favors by *always* waiting for you, changing their plans, or missing out on movies or concerts just because you fail to show up. If your friend says, "To hell with finals! Let's go skiing this weekend. We can study Sunday night for awhile," you don't have to think it's a great idea, and you certainly don't have to go. Friendships that can't weather some differences in opinions or interests aren't worth much.

What *does* it mean to hang around with people who like you, warts and all? Better yet, what does it feel like? It feels *safe*. It feels *comfortable*. It feels *good.* Do you have to be accountable from time to time? Sure. A good friend won't always be there for you because that isn't possible. A good friend will have her own life, too. There will be times when she can't be there for you. And, a good friend won't let you abuse or neglect her. If you start treating her poorly, a good friend will let the relationship cool off for awhile. If it's your parents, you'll probably have to be accountable more than you'd like. No matter how many power struggles you may have about chores or curfews, when all is said and done you won't feel diminished by the corrective feedback or limits that your parents impose—you'll eventually feel cared for.

Finding people whom we can trust and with whom we can share our deepest secrets and feelings is a cornerstone of emotional health and power. Learning to do this comfortably takes at least until we're in our early thirties. The sooner you begin, the sooner you'll know how to find them.

15

Getting Healthy Power

The highest proof of virtue is to possess bound-
less power without abusing it.

—T. B. Macaulay, *The Life and Writings of Addison,* 1843

People have become awfully confused about power
lately. We feel sorry for people who perpetrate, and we
blame the victim. Then, we turn around after someone vic-
timizes us and we try to perpetrate to make up for it. No
wonder we're confused. To help you get a sense of where the
middle ground lies on this dimension, we'd like to start
with a couple of definitions. St. Paul psychologists James
Maddock and Noel Larson wrote:

*Power is the capacity to influence. Power is the energy of
life, literally and figuratively moving out and taking up*

space in the world. Control can be defined most simply as a reciprocal to power, that is, as the capacity to restrain or regulate influence. *Control is the boundedness of life, recognized in the inevitable limitations on everything that exists. In our view, power and control are interactive concepts that can be understood best in relation to each other. Defined in this way, a deeper meaning arises out of the tension between them, and the terms can be combined into a single dialectical construct:* power/control.[28]

Power and control can be either good or bad depending on the situation and how they are exercised. If you get me to vote for you by threatening to break my legs, that's power, but it isn't the kind we admire. If I take up your cause because I am so deeply moved by both the wisdom of your words and the courage of your actions, then we're talking about power of another sort.

If you keep going into my closet and borrowing my clothes despite my protests, then I will feel powerless after awhile. If I don't ever control this intrusion, I never say "no" to you because I'm afraid that I will lose your friendship if I do, then obviously I am allowing you to have excessive power in our relationship.

If I widen my circle of friends so that I'm not putting all of my eggs in one basket, then I will also increase my power within our relationship. In a relationship where the power is out of balance, the person who wants or needs the relationship *less* has more power.

Put Up Yer Dukes? Fergeddaboudit!

There are people who come into therapy with one word that describes them: tough. Because we believe that all human behavior has a reason beneath it, we have to ask ourselves, "How does that tough exterior help her?" As we get to know the person, it becomes clear. Whether you're old or young, male or female, Caucasian or Asian or African-American, the purpose of "tough" is protection. Adults and teenagers often confuse toughness and healthy power. A tough person can be powerful in the sense of getting what she wants by intimidating others, but it's pretty hard to get what we need from others when we have that tough exterior shield up most of the time. It is heartwarming, then, to see people begin to trust and let that cloak of anger relax a little in their therapy process. As they do, it is exciting to witness them acquiring real power.

Seventeen-year-old Tom has a friend, Ed, who always tries to get him into a huge argument about something. For some reason, Ed has mistakenly learned that the best way to feel connected to others is to debate and argue with them. No matter what the topic, Ed always manages to turn it into a conflict. Tom says, "What a gorgeous day! The air is so clean and fresh, the sky is blue."

Ed interrupts, "Well, it's not exactly blue-blue. It's more a pale blue."

Tom says, "I really enjoyed that movie."

Instead of asking, "What did you like about it?" which would keep the conversation going, Ed says, "I didn't. It was too superficial for me. I can't believe you liked it.

What's wrong with you?" This pretty much kills their interaction.

Tom has decided that he wants a change in the friendship. He musters up the courage to tactfully tell Ed that he wishes Ed wasn't so argumentative. Ed just argues with Tom about how he isn't argumentative. Ed says he's just a critical thinker who likes to analyze things, and he's always thought that Tom was a lightweight when it came to "using his head" in these matters. Tom is befuddled. At first it feels like his only two options are to continue to put up with it or to end the relationship, but Tom is acquiring some emotional intelligence. He's beginning to see that there may be some middle ground here. He sees that *his* part is that he bites the bait, so to speak, and then complains when the hook cuts through his cheek. He thinks about this for a few days, and then he decides that it's worth a try. He decides to *move in* when Ed is being critical instead of moving away.

From what ensued, you'd think the sky had opened up and the hand of God had touched the two of them. Ed and Tom were on the way to school one morning when Tom said, "I was really shocked and disgusted when that story broke last night about the teacher who was sexually abusing kids at our old junior high. I shuddered just to think about it."

Trying to show how tough he is, and how startling things don't startle him, Ed replied, "You're too sensitive. It happens all the time. The world is a mean place sometimes. Get over it, buddy."

Instead of becoming defensive or questioning Ed's sensitivity, and escalating it into an argument, Tom simply created an opening to convert it into a mutual conversation by *moving in* rather than away. "Yes, I see your point." Tom paused for a moment, and then continued, "I wonder what is broken about a man who molests children?" Brilliant. He *affirmed* Ed without agreeing with him. Then he *took control* (i.e., used power) to move the conversation past the potential flash point.

Just for a nanosecond, Ed was stunned. Being a know-it-all, he had to think fast to make up a reasonable-sounding reply. "Uh . . . he's probably a sick SOB. Just a sick SOB."

It was a pretty lame answer, but Tom didn't focus on that. He tried to protect Ed's dignity without encouraging any further combativeness. "Yes. He'd have to be a sick SOB." Tom paused for another second and then went on, "I wonder what would make someone that sick?" He was moving it forward again, away from the *field of combat* and into the *realm of conversation.* Ed was growing quiet. The anxiety that underlies people who are excessively defensive was seeping through to the surface. Tom felt that, so he didn't wait for a reply. He did not want to make Ed more uncomfortable than he was already becoming. "I mean, I wonder if he was molested or beaten or something when he was a kid? Do you think that's a possibility?" He left Ed an easy opening with an easy reply.

Ed said, "Maybe so. I don't know. Could be."

It was a masterful interchange. The emotional tone in the car had gone from tense and ominous to calm and relaxed in a matter of seconds, and all because Tom had *chosen* to exert healthy power rather than become a victim of Ed's intimidation, and rather than intimidating back. Instead of "putting up his dukes" and slugging it out with Ed, Tom chose to do the following:

One Powerful Way to Handle Argumentative People

Critical, Defensive or Combative Statement	Affirm Without Agreeing, Move It Forward into Conversation
"You liked *that* movie? What's *wrong* with you?"	"Yes, in fact, I loved it. Isn't that a riot? I *never* thought I'd hear myself say *that!*"
"You're *always* late for *everything*."	"I do have a problem with being on time. I'm working on it, though. I was on time four out of seven times this week because I keep a reminder in my shirt pocket at all times."
"Well, the sky isn't exactly blue. It's actually a pale blue."	"Yes. I see. I just *love* days like this! It's such a gorgeous day!"
"You were *scared* when that police car zipped by us? *I* wasn't."	"Yes, my startle response tends to be a little stronger than most. My pediatrician even noted that when I was an infant. Isn't it interesting how different each person is?"

The ability to defuse tense interpersonal interactions is one of the most important aspects of emotional intelligence. It often separates those who are moderately successful and adjusted in life from those who are very much so. It is also a key element of healthy power, as we hope we have just demonstrated. Equally important is the closely related ability to carry on a civil conversation. We consult with scores of businesses, large and small, and are constantly reminded by executives and managers that young adults who haven't learned to converse are at a distinct disadvantage when it comes to hiring and promotions. Even if you're clumsy at it in the beginning, the more you practice what we have outlined above, the better the rest of your life will be.

16

Facing the Serious Stuff

We know ourselves so little that many think
they are going to die when they are well, and many
think they are well when they are near dying.

—Blaise Pascal, *Pensées,* XXV, 1670

Teenagers, like everyone else, are susceptible to problems. Things that we, the authors, consider serious and
things that you consider serious may not be the same. We
simply want everyone to know that the problems listed here
and in chapter 8 do not easily resolve themselves. They
often require support from others, if not outright professional help. Also, we always caution our clients against the
search for a quick fix—there is no such thing. Resolving
most human problems means making a change, and making changes takes time because it involves replacing old
habits with new ones. Nobody ever sat down in a car with

a manual transmission and started driving smoothly. It takes time and effort to learn how to use the clutch and gas pedal simultaneously. Last, in addition to having the courage to admit a serious problem, beware of overdiagnosis. While some alcoholics deny their problem until the day they die, not everyone who gets in over her head with alcohol is an alcoholic.

Addictions

When a child becomes a teenager, it would be good if parents could say something like the following: "We know that you may experiment with drinking or other chemicals as you go through adolescence. We want you to know three things. *First,* we don't want you to drive any vehicle while under the influence, and we don't want you to ride with someone who is under the influence. If either of those is about to happen, either call us or call a cab, and we'll take care of it. We won't get mad. *Second,* we do not allow under-age people to drink in our home. It is illegal, inappropriate and just plain stupid in today's litigious society. If you or anyone you bring into or let into our home uses while here, there will be appropriate consequences. *Third,* addiction is a fact of life for many people. It happens to the best of us. If we see that you're going under because of an addiction, we will not let you down. We will reach down, give you a hand up, and gently but firmly put you into treatment. *There is no reason for anyone in America to suffer with an untreated addiction in the twenty-first century."*

If your parents haven't said these things to you, we encourage you to make a copy of the above paragraph and give it to them. They can read it aloud to you, word-for-word, if need be. There is nothing artificial about doing it this way, if they can learn to mean it sincerely. Sometimes having the right words to say is the only thing getting in one's way. Don't be afraid to help them out with the words.

We have been delightfully stunned by the number of teenagers and young adults who have come into therapy with us after going to their parents and saying, "Mom, Dad, I'm struggling with some things. I was wondering if I could go see a counselor?" It is often during their first session that they say they may be in over their heads with drugs or alcohol, but they don't know how to deal with the consequences of admitting it. Sometimes they are afraid of their parents getting angry, or they are afraid of their parents' fear, guilt, shame or self-blame, which can sometimes be worse. It is much easier to talk about difficult problems with someone who is grown-up enough to listen to *you* rather than become preoccupied with their own anxiety and discomfort about what you're telling them. In those cases, having a more objective ally, like a therapist, can make it much easier to bring these things up with parents.

If you believe that you are struggling with an addiction, you might want to ask yourself how many of the following signs or symptoms you have:

1. *Preoccupation*—This includes thinking about using more and more, and planning your activities and life around using.

2. *Increased tolerance*—Needing to use more and more to
   have an effect, and being able to handle more and
   more without appearing to be intoxicated. People
   often brag about how much they can drink or use. In
   99.9 percent of these cases, the person bragging is
   already an alcoholic or addict.

3. *Loss of control*—This includes saying you're going to
   use less tonight than you usually do, and then trick-
   ing yourself into not sticking with your vow. Also,
   and this shocks many adults with whom we work, if
   you have ever tried to quit using a chemical or doing
   some other compulsive behavior, you are acknowledging that it's a problem. Quitting or cutting back
   doesn't cross the minds of nonaddicts because they
   don't have a problem in the first place. You would
   only want to cut back or quit if you had a problem.

4. *Moodiness*—People get moody now and then. Teenagers
   supposedly are moody more often than adults are.
   People who are gradually becoming addicted to something get moody more than they normally would. If
   you're becoming a pain in the rear end to be around,
   and you're using mood-altering chemicals regularly,
   consider the possibility that something is gnawing at
   you from the inside out rather than from the outside in.

5. *Hiding/shame*—We have worked with countless families where one of the teenagers and one of the parents
   are alcoholic. Everyone "secretly" knows it, but
   nobody wants to say anything because they're all
   embarrassed and afraid. Although it isn't funny while
   it's happening, after these families have healed for a

few years, they recognize the strange and often humorous circumstances under which they have been living. The two alcoholics can smile and shake their heads in wonderment about how they each used to sneak into the liquor cabinet at night and take a few stiff hits off the whiskey bottle, all the while noticing how the level in the bottle was declining faster than it should have been because the other person was doing the same thing. Oh, the tangled webs we weave.

Eating Disorders

Anorexia and bulimia are life-threatening problems that have some of the same compulsive, ritualized features as addictions. We live in a culture that encourages eating disorders by emphasizing *over*eating on the one hand and emphasizing unrealistic physical appearance on the other. It's a terrible double bind. More girls and women have these disorders, but boys and men are not immune to them. The fear and shame connected with the bingeing and purging of bulimia often prevent the person from seeking help. With anorexia, the rigid desire to control one's eating along with the metaphorical refusal to live that accompanies the refusal to eat make it one of the most life-threatening illnesses, and one of the hardest to treat. People die from anorexia and bulimia.

In *Reviving Ophelia,* Mary Pipher noted that in 1951, Miss Sweden was five feet, seven inches tall and weighed 151 pounds. In 1983, Miss Sweden was five feet, nine inches tall and weighed 109 pounds. She went on to say, "Studies report that on any given day in America, half our teenage girls are dieting and that one in five young women has an eating disorder. Eight million women have eating disorders in America."[29]

Obsessive-Compulsive Disorder (OCD)

Being orderly and organized is usually a good thing. Being haunted and trapped by rituals or thoughts that are seemingly beyond your control is not a good thing. The more obvious cases of OCD seem to have a learned and/or anxiety-reducing component in addition to their biological cause, with the latter being related to certain areas of the brain involved with repetitive behavior. Some dogs, for example, may have a compulsive aspect to their grooming behavior forcing them to lick themselves uncontrollably until their hair is pulled out. Researchers have narrowed this behavior down to the part of the brain responsible for this instinctual grooming pattern. It is possible that a similar mechanism is responsible for at least *some* aspects of OCD in humans.

OCD can be treated with cognitive-behavioral therapy, in which your own inner speech and thinking is used to stop the repetitive behavior. Learning relaxation strategies helps, as does deeper psychotherapy around the anxiety that may be driving the compulsive behavior or obsessive thinking. In many cases, symptoms also respond well to SSRIs, the antidepressants that help to maintain adequate serotonin levels like Prozac and its cousins. OCD is very treatable.

Cutting

One of the national news programs did a segment on teenagers and young adults who "cut" themselves regularly. They did a good job of investigating the problem and explaining its causes and some of the treatments. As part of their investigation, they presented the case of a teenager who was admitted to an inpatient psychiatric hospital in the 1990s, and who was subsequently released as "untreatable." The hospital staff apparently did not understand the origins of or treatments for this fairly common problem. We were surprised, to say the least, because this symptom has been identified and treated for quite a long time.

Cutting is usually a response to some pretty severe distress or trauma within the family. It is believed to be a way for the person to either (1) confirm that his own physical boundaries still exist, or (2) unconsciously create a distraction from a more painful emotional injury deep inside oneself. It can become as driven and addictive as drug or alcohol dependency, and often requires professional help to resolve the underlying trauma.

Suicide

In 1996, more teenagers and young adults died of suicide than from cancer, heart disease, AIDS, birth defects, stroke, pneumonia and influenza, and chronic lung disease combined. In 1996, suicide was the second-leading cause of death among college students, the third-leading cause of death among those aged fifteen to twenty-four years, and the fourth-leading cause of death among those aged ten to fourteen years. From 1980 to 1996, the rate of suicide among African-American males aged fifteen to nineteen years increased by 105 percent. It is a hopeful sign that while the incidence of suicide among adolescents and young adults nearly tripled from 1965 to 1987, teen suicide rates in the past ten years have actually been declining, possibly due to increased recognition and treatment. [30]

Any suicide threat should be taken seriously, and it is especially important to know that talking about suicide does not increase the likelihood that someone will kill himself. Current cognitive-behavioral research on suicide suggests that the key emotional factor in suicide is a feeling of hopelessness. People can be depressed, sad, blue, "down," you name it, but when they start to feel hopeless, they are at much higher risk of suicide. What would make any of us more hopeless than the feeling and belief that you are totally alone? This includes the feeling that no one can see "the real you" and that you can't talk to those close to you because they either tell you not to worry, they try to fix it, they get really uncomfortable themselves or they get mad. Faith and hope flow directly out of relationship, out of emotional connection.

Homicide

The United States has by far the highest homicide rate of any of the industrialized nations. Young adults are at the greatest risk of being murdered, representing 60 percent of all victims. Males are three quarters of all victims. The rates for teenage boys are at a record high. Half of the offenders are between fifteen and twenty-four. For nonwhite males ages fifteen to nineteen, homicide rates in 1990 were 92 per 100,000. For whites, the number was 13 per 100,000. Homicide rates for black male teenagers more than doubled between 1985 and 1990. For children under age fourteen, current homicide rates are at near-record highs. *On the positive side, the preliminary age-adjusted homicide rate fell 12 percent in 1997.*

As a teen reading this book, we ask that you reflect on what it means to you personally to be a citizen of the most homicidal industrialized nation on earth. Then, you should refer back to the earlier parts of this book dealing with impulse control, feelings, dissociation and power, among others. Remember that you have to be in some kind of disconnected, dissociated state to be able to kill another human being. Remember that people who are emotionally isolated from one another are more likely to be dissociated. Remember that it is always possible to repair the connections between people, if you are willing to risk embarrassment and discomfort.

Suffering Abuse

This is a difficult one for many adults to accept, but once they do their lives become a lot better. It is not an accident that some people get into one abusive relationship after another. It can be an accident in the very beginning of one's dating history, but people from really healthy families quickly learn how to spot the subtle cues given off by people who have the potential to be abusive. The problem is that people from not-so-healthy families wear blinders that prevent them from picking up the cues that are there until it's too late. Then those same blinders keep the person in the relationship much longer than is healthy. Blinders can be permanently removed by maintaining small changes over a period of months. The first time you get out of a scary relationship *early on,* it will feel wrong. The next time, it won't feel quite so wrong. The third time, it will feel sad, but not wrong.

If someone you're out with is scary—if they continually make nasty comments or threaten violence—then you can be assured that they have the potential for abuse. Being scary *is* abusive by itself. Teenagers from healthy families have a template in their heads that says, "I know what a safe person looks like. I know what it feels like to be emotionally and physically safe." When they are around someone who isn't so safe, that person sticks out like a sore thumb. A teenager from a family that isn't so safe—one that has a lot of spoiling and babying, alcoholism, physical or emotional neglect or abuse, etc.—has a template that says, "Oh, I've been around *this* stuff before. This isn't so bad. I can handle *this.*" When they are around someone who isn't safe, that person feels familiar. *That's* the blinder. It can be removed.

Abusing Others

If you scare people with your anger, if you intimidate people, if you are controlling, pushy or violent, let yourself become aware of the *fear, hurt* or *shame* that underlies your anger. If you can't identify it or if you think we are crazy for suggesting it, then we encourage you to do something about that blinder before it gets you into serious legal difficulties. If you doubt that you'll ever get into legal difficulties, we assure you that you will have serious relationship problems until you deal with this. It is absolutely unavoidable.

Remember that anger is there to protect us. When our anger gets us into trouble regularly, it is almost always a signal that it is *we* who are out of step, not the rest of the world. Of course, if your anger is getting you into trouble a lot, you will believe that it's everyone else who is causing the problems. This isn't likely.

In Conclusion

We have long spoken and written about the courageous process that we call *uncovering and admitting.* The step between hiding in shame and seeking help can seem like an impossible leap across the Grand Canyon. If you stop and think about it for a moment, if you look at the people around you or watch television or read newspapers, you will see that millions of people, famous and not, have taken that very manageable step to deal with their "secret" problem.

A colleague told us about her own uncovering and admitting process. She said that her fear of being "found out" was so great and her shame about being a helping professional with a serious problem was so deep that the only way she was able to take that step was to sit down and write out what became a long list of all the people she knew who had the same problem. She began with politicians, actors and other public figures whom she knew had the problem. Then she started moving into her own world, listing business associates and people in her field. Finally, she listed the few friends and family members who had the problem. Then she set the list aside for twenty-four hours. When she returned to look at it the next day, what stood out was how she would be "okay" because every single person on her list had taken that step, and they were all "okay," too.

Then she picked up the phone and made the call that changed her life forever.

17

Finding an Identity

Life is a series of surprises.

—Ralph Waldo Emerson, *Circles,* 1841

Filling in the Stages

When someone comes to a psychologist for help with a problem, it is often very important for the therapist to have a framework in her head for the developmental strengths and shortages that the client brings in. Imagine a cup that can be filled to any level. Then imagine that all of your life experiences from birth until young adulthood are what determine how full that cup is. The emotional-health level of that cup is determined by all of the love or lack of it, structure or lack of it, teaching, support, abandonment, criticism and encouragement you receive while growing up.

In chapter 9, we said that we used Erik Erikson's stages as our developmental framework because it is so useful in helping people figure out where they're stuck. If we have an apparently competent thirty-two-year-old professional man before us who says that the only person in his life that he can really rely on in any personal sense is his wife or girlfriend, then it is possible that he may have some trust problems. After all, if every one of those emotional support eggs is in one basket, that basket is going to be heavily weighed down. If a forty-seven-year-old woman says that she'd like to go back to school and finish up the bachelor's degree she set aside years ago after her first child was born, but that she can't seem to get past the overwhelming guilt that plagues her at the thought of her husband making a couple of his own meals during the week, then perhaps she is struggling with an initiative-versus-guilt dilemma.

We would like to share with you some of the tidbits of development that have been particularly helpful to our clients. For each of Erikson's first five developmental stages, we will simply list some of the indicators of having filled in that part of the cup. You may be able to see some of these in yourself. As you read through them, remember that this is not just a way to measure a shortage in yourself. Each item on the list represents a goal or a marker on the road map to healthy adulthood.

Trust versus Mistrust

1. I know the world has dangers in it, but in general I feel okay and safe.

2. There are people with whom I can share "the real me."

3. During times of crisis, I know whom I can lean on for support.

4. I believe that, despite all our flaws, human beings basically mean well.

Autonomy versus Shame and Doubt

1. I have a very different opinion about the death penalty than my friends do.

2. My boyfriend wants me to have sex with him, but I told him I wasn't ready.

3. I went to that movie by myself. Nobody else wanted to go.

4. My feelings about this are okay, even though they're different from yours.

Initiative versus Guilt

1. I just went down there and applied for a job.

2. I washed the car. Do you think I could use it this afternoon?

3. I've decided to go to college in New Hampshire. Yes, I know it's far away.

4. I asked everyone in the neighborhood if I could mow their lawns for five dollars.

Competence versus Inferiority

1. I like the fact that I play hockey well.

2. I want to learn how to put together a five-course Northern Italian meal.

3. Believe it or not, I get a kick out of completing these algebra problems.

4. Dad, I like it when you teach me things.

Identity versus Identity Confusion

1. I changed majors twice before I realized that literature was my true passion.

2. I'm not always sure where I'll wind up when I'm in my thirties, but I feel like I'm on a good path for now and that what I learn now will be useful to me later in life, regardless.

3. I am definitely good at tennis, but when it comes to math, I definitely have to work harder than most.

4. I'm beginning to feel like there is a real "me" inside. I don't have *quite* as much anxiety about who I am as I did last year.

Keeping at It

People who can acknowledge the weak spots in their developmental building blocks are eventually able to fill them in. People who are too scared or ashamed to do so became stuck. The good news is that no matter how old you are, it is never too late to get back in and start filling in those gaps. No one *ever* fills in these stages completely or perfectly, so that is not the issue. The goal is to fill each one in *enough* so that you can build on it from the next level without the whole thing collapsing. It is very typical and very normal for people to enter their twenties with a couple of major shortages. More and more, we see young adults coming in to do some "identity clarification work," or to "fill in the gaps," as many of them call it, in their mid- to late twenties.

What you do to fill in those gaps will depend in part on how large the gaps are. If the weak spot in your trust building block stems from not having a broad enough base of emotional support (all your eggs in one basket), then joining some kind of activity, like a social or service group may be all that you need to do. If the gap is bigger and you have a mistrust of people, then joining a support group or therapy group may be the answer. We offer several therapy groups in our practice because a large number of otherwise successful Americans have a pretty narrow base of emotional support. A therapy group is often the most effective way to teach people how to fill in this gap.

Whatever the weak spots in your development, you can be assured that they can be filled in . . . if you keep at it.

18

Staking Out the Extremes

There is a mean in all things; there are, in short,
certain fixed limits, on either side
of which what is right cannot exist.

—Horace, *Satires,* I, c. 25 B.C.

The *Minnesota Multiphasic Personality Inventory (MMPI-2)* is the most widely used psychological test of clinical syndromes in the world. It has been translated into countless languages, and there are now nearly sixty years of research data to help support and interpret its scales. There is a separate adolescent version of the test—the MMPI-A—because adolescents who take the adult version wind up looking . . . well . . . pretty unhealthy. Being an adolescent *isn't* unhealthy, it's just different, so they constructed another test with different norms more suitable for teens.

In other words, there *are* some important personality

differences between adolescents and adults, and for any of us to pretend otherwise would be silly. Mary Pipher wrote, "The emotional system is immature in early adolescence. Emotions are extreme and changeable. Small events can trigger enormous reactions. A negative comment about appearance or a bad mark on a test can hurl a teenager into despair."[31] As mentioned in an earlier chapter, some of this is due to brain differences between adolescents and adults.

Faulty Filters

What can a teenager do about these emotional storms and this tendency toward overreaction? Part of it simply changes as she moves out of the teen years. Another part will begin to change as a result of learning better ways to look at the world. The filters through which we interpret the world are a significant factor in how healthy we eventually become. If everything passes through a "victim filter," then the world is a pretty hostile and dangerous place. If it all passes through a "perpetrator filter," then everything in the world becomes "easy pickings." Of course, many people don't like you when all is said and done because nobody likes to get ripped off.

If everything passes through a filter that says, "When something bad happens to me, it means life will *always* be bad for me," then life becomes a pretty miserable place to be. After all, "bad" things happen to *everybody* now and then because life isn't perfect. If getting a flat tire is a signal the entire remainder of your life will be awful, then we don't need you to explain why you're feeling so awful. If that were true, we'd feel awful, too. If you have faulty filters, you may be stuck in the storms of adolescence long after your friends have moved on into their adult lives. Your friend has fixed her flat tire and is getting on with her day proud of the fact that she was able to fix the flat "in no time flat." You, on the other hand, are standing by the side of the road raging at the tire and shaking your fist at the sky, convinced that life as you knew it is over for good.

Given that how we filter life is such an important part of how we feel, wouldn't it be wonderful if there were a way to remove the old faulty filters and install new, functional ones? There is. Cognitive behavioral psychologists like Aaron Beck, Martin Seligman, Albert Ellis, David Burns and Christine Padesky have developed very effective tools to help you do just that. We especially like Burns' *The New Mood Therapy,* Seligman's *Learned Optimism* and Greenberger's and Padesky's infinitely useful workbook *Mind over Mood.*

To give you a sampling of how this would work, let's look at some extreme thinking and what you might do about it. Let's say that you and your best friend just had a fight. As you walk into your house at the end of the school day, you feel like your entire world is collapsing around you. You're scared, your heart is racing, you feel like you've been kicked in the gut, you wish you could just disappear off the face of the earth, you're depressed, empty, mad as a wet hen, lonely, hurt. Your emotions are swirling around in your body like the plague.

In a case like this, you should pull out a lined notebook, legal pad or journal page, and at the top of it you write:

Sharon and I just had a fight, and . . .

Then you open the floodgates in your head and just let her rip! Write down everything that comes to mind without worrying whether it's true or makes sense. You might write:

I'll never see her again.

I'll never have another best friend.

I'll be alone the rest of my life.

Everyone will hear about it and be talking about me.

I'm going to die.

I'm a failure at relationships.

My parents will think I'm crazy or sick.

My parents will be crushed—they can't handle it when I'm sad.

Then, pick the consequence that bothers you the most. Write the situation and the consequence you fear at the top of a new page:

Sharon and I just had a fight, and I'll never see her again.

Beneath this statement, begin to list the *facts* that dispute this *faulty filtering system*:

My sister had a bad fight with her best friend, and they're still good friends.

Sharon and I had a fight at camp last year and hardly did anything with each other while there, but when we got back home we made up and got along great the rest of the summer.

I'll see Sharon at school tomorrow even if we don't speak to each other.

Sharon and I have been best friends since preschool, and like all long-term friendships, we've had our ups and downs.

Martin Seligman calls this the "disputation" phase, in which you dispute the mistaken belief. Christine Padesky calls it listing the "evidence that does not support the hot thought." This may seem corny or lame, but this method is one of the most heavily researched. It has proven to be one of the most powerful therapeutic techniques that people can use to improve their moods, decrease depression and anxiety, and improve relationships.

The next time you find yourself tossed around in a frightening hurricane of conflicting and painful emotions, try this. It's pretty amazing how much our childhood filters determine how we frame the everyday events in our lives. Everyone knows that best friends fight. This is normal. When you're in the middle of the hurricane, it's hard to see if you're near land or hundreds of miles out to sea. Taking out those filters and cleaning them, or replacing them with new ones, can make all the difference in the world.

Part IV

Bringing It
All Back Home

19

And in the End . . .

Hope springs exulting on triumphant wing.

—Robert Burns, *The Cotter's Saturday Night*, 1785

Following the sad death of John F. Kennedy Jr., Joan Ryan wrote about our continued fascination with the 1960s in a *San Francisco Sunday Examiner and Chronicle* essay entitled "Lost Era, Lost Illusions." She cited several readers' letters, including one by a man who wrote that JFK Jr. reminds us "of a time when men and women were called on to make decisions," such as Vietnam, civil rights and the Cold War. The man went on to say that JFK Jr.'s death also reminds us "that we have a connection to something heroic that elevates why we are here on Earth to something more meaningful than whether to purchase the SUV or home in the 'burbs." [32]

When the chips are down and things are so painful that

people start to talk about what's really going on with them instead of pretending like they're living in reruns of *Father Knows Best* or *The Brady Bunch,* what we hear most often from parents and children is that they are so stressed and isolated that they don't seem to be connected to much at all. In his heartfelt bestseller, *The Greatest Generation, NBC News* anchor Tom Brokaw respectfully elevated to epic proportions the everyday, ordinary, and therefore extraordinary, heroism of the men and women who helped this nation make it through World War II. In that same book, he wisely pointed out that the children of those World War II heroes paid a dear price for those war-damaged, emotionally repressed parents raising them. Life is rarely black-and-white.

In concluding her reflections on the death of JFK Jr., Joan Ryan wrote, "As I read the letters, I thought about how young people today are trying to re-create the decade, even holding another Woodstock. It's sad to watch, but I admit I went through a similar stage myself. Perhaps someday soon, we'll have a generation that finally stops looking over its shoulder at better times and, breaking free from cynicism, writes a new American fairy tale."[33]

Indeed, there *are* some things to think about here. The 1990s were filled with painfully exquisite contradictions. We saw nearly unexplainable economic growth and decreases in unemployment. At the same time, the number of people falling below the poverty level was either maintained or continued to increase, depending on how you measure poverty. We saw people almost obsessed with personal growth and spirituality at the same time that loneliness, alienation, violence and impulsivity reached epidemic proportions. Psychologists acknowledge that the number of personality disorders—serious, long-term emotional problems—has increased even though our ability to treat emotional problems has improved dramatically over the past fifty years.

The presence of contradictions produces anxiety. Anxiety is uncomfortable. Resolving contradictions reduces anxiety. So, we hurry to find resolutions to the contradictions in the hopes of reducing our anxiety. Because human beings are flawed, we often overshoot the mark and wind up creating an equal but opposite problem. At other times, we respond to our ambivalence by harking back to an earlier era, being careful to mythologize it in our minds first so that our image of it is truly like a fairy tale.

We aren't convinced that this is all bad, though. If young people want to hold another Woodstock, how is that any different from old people having a Roaring Twenties party or conducting Civil War reenactments? One of the ways we find the meaning in history is to reenact parts of it. By so doing, we are able to experience and assimilate it in a less sterile, abstract, academic way. Perhaps it is sad that young people held another Woodstock because it meant they were yearning for better days that had long gone by; or perhaps it is just an excellent way to make sense of the past—to embrace it—in preparation for the new dreams that are already incubating in their unconscious minds.

History tells us that there will always be Vietnams, Cold Wars or Civil Rights Movements in one arena or another because that is what a continually evolving society includes—problems to be acknowledged and solved. The contradictions of the 1990s were painfully exquisite, but we're putting our money on the next generation coming up from the ranks, and then the one after that, and the one after that.

We hope that you have found something of value in this book to help you accomplish just that.

APPENDIX:
WHY SEVEN?

Every once in a while someone comes along and has such a comprehensive impact on your life that you don't see it for a long, long time. When I was a sophomore in college, I was wondering what I was supposed to be doing with my life and feeling the need to declare a major. I found myself gravitating toward law more than anything else because I admired my father and the remarkable integrity he displayed in his law career. That preliminary plan served its purpose: to give me *something* to say when people asked what I was going to do with my life. Towards the end of that year, however, I found the excellence of two of my professors grabbing and pulling me headlong into psychology. One of the professors was a clinician who knew how to truly connect with college students. The other was an experimental psychologist whose enthusiastic, playful love of research and experimentation was infectious to many of his students, including me.

I declared a psychology major that spring.

By the time my final year rolled around, we were required to do a senior research experiment in psychology, and I knew exactly what I wanted to do. This energetic professor had somehow managed to get many of us excited by the brand new field of information processing, in which concepts from the infant field of computer science were being used to help us understand human thinking and memory. In 1956, George A. Miller wrote one of the most famous journal articles in the history of psychology for the prestigious *Psychological Review*. The title of the article was "The Magic Number Seven, Plus or Minus Two: Some Limits on Our Capacity for Processing Information."

The "magic number seven" refers to the channel capacity, or the amount of information that a human being can process simultaneously. The key word here is "simultaneously." It can also be described as the number of chunks of information that we can keep in short-term memory at one given moment. For example, if you tell someone a phone number, and they don't have a pen and paper to write it down, most people are able to remember seven numbers. One of the subtests on the Wechsler Adult Intelligence Scale-Revised is called Digit Span. The test administrator reads increasingly long lists of digits, and your task is to repeat them back right away. The average number that people can repeat correctly is "seven, plus or minus two."

If you use a mnemonic device, such as rehearsing the list immediately or visualizing the numbers in "chunks" of two or three, then you can usually remember more. The effects of this "chunking" can be seen with telephone numbers. If you already know your area code, you don't have to memorize that when the number is given to you by the operator, because "651" or "520" is now *one* number to you. If you know your area code and seven-digit phone number, then adding a four-digit password for a calling card is a piece of cake. All you really have to remember is "my entire phone number" plus "3791." The magic number is "seven, plus or minus two" because the range for most human beings is from five to nine. That's what I did my senior research project on, and it was the beginning of a lifelong love of the scientific side of psychology. Most of the clinical side came later.

The number "seven" is one of those Biblical numbers. It appears with significance in almost every culture. There it was popping up as one of the most significant pieces of research and experimental thought of the mid- to late 1900s. When it comes to complex stimuli, like people's faces, complex tastes and smells, or complex emotions, human beings can remember many more than seven. If you think about it when it comes to lists, though, seven is about the limit of what people are willing or able to handle. A list of seven, like seven shades of gray, seven different sizes of circles or squares, or seven gradations on a rating scale (from "one = never" to "seven = always") is able to keep our attention because we are able to keep its seven elements in mind all at one time. In other words, a list of seven often allows the reader to form a single, coherent mental picture. Linda and I hope that a coherent picture of smart teenagers moving into healthy adulthood comes across in this book.

So we have seven, that magic number. Thanks to Lawrence E. Murphy, Ph.D., for being the first of many to delight my mind with the wonders of psychology.

John C. Friel, Ph.D.

ENDNOTES

1. Barbara Kantrowitz and Pat Wingert, "How Well Do You Know Your Kids?" *Newsweek,* 10 May 1999, 36–40.
2. Ibid.
3. Miles Corwin, "Mother Turns Grief, Grit to Memorial for Slain Son," *Los Angeles Times,* 29 October 1995, A27–A28.
4. Ibid.
5. *Mother Teresa,* dir. Ann Petrie and Jeanette Petrie, 82 min., Petrie Productions, 1985, videocassette.
6. John Friel solely wrote this chapter.
7. Martin E. P. Seligman, *Learned Optimism: How to Change Your Mind and Your Life* (New York: Alfred A. Knopf, 1991).
8. Sylvia Rimm, *Dr. Sylvia Rimm's Smart Parenting: How to Parent So Children Will Learn* (New York: Crown Publishers, 1996), 8.
9. Statistics in the above paragraphs were adapted from Charles Sykes, *Dumbing Down Our Kids* (St. Martin's Griffin, New York, 1996).

10. Mary Pipher, *Reviving Ophelia: Saving the Selves of Adolescent Girls* (New York: Ballantine Books, 1995), 64.

11. Ibid.

12. Nancy Ann Jeffrey, "Bratlash," *The Wall Street Journal,* reprinted in the *Minneapolis Star Tribune,* 22 January 2000, E1–E2.

13. Ibid, E2.

14. William Doherty, *Take Back Your Kids: Confident Parenting in Turbulent Times* (Notre Dame, Ind.: Sorin Books, 2000).

15. Gershen Kaufman, *Shame: The Power of Caring* (Cambridge: Schenkman Publishing Company, 1980).

16. Dean Ornish, *Love and Survival: The Scientific Basis for the Healing Power of Intimacy* (New York: HarperCollins, 1998).

17. Barbara Kantrowitz and Pat Wingert, "How Well Do You Know Your Kids?" *Newsweek,* 10 May 1999, 36–40.

18. Ellen Galinsky, *Ask the Children: What America's Children Really Think About Working Parents* (New York: William Morrow & Co., 1999).

19. Peter Johnson, "Secret Service Opens Up in School Shootings Report," *USA Today,* 14 March 2000.

20. David J. Spiegel, R. Bloom, H. C. Kraemer and E. Gottheil, "Effect of Psychosocial Treatment on Survival of Patients with Metastatic Breast Cancer," *The Lancet* ii (1989): 888–891.

21. Farnum Gray, Paul S. Graubard and Harry Rosenberg,

"Little Brother Is Changing You," *Psychology Today,*
March 1974: 42–46.

22. Martin E. P. Seligman, *Learned Optimism: How to
Change Your Mind and Your Life* (New York: Alfred A.
Knopf, 1991), 18.

23. Ibid, 18.

24. From an *ABCNews.com* report on December 13, 1999.

25. Robert Frey, personal communication, 1987.

26. Stanley Milgram, "Behavioral Study of Obedience,"
Journal of Personality and Social Psychology 67 (1963):
371–378.

27. John Steinbeck, *Cannery Row* (New York: Viking
Press, 1945).

28. James W. Maddock and Noel R. Larson, *Incestuous
Families: An Ecological Approach to Understanding and
Treatment* (New York: W. W. Norton & Co., 1995),
55.

29. Mary Pipher, *Reviving Ophelia: Saving the Selves of
Adolescent Girls* (New York: Ballantine Books, 1995).

30. The quote is from the National Alliance for the
Mentally Ill, *www.nami.org.*

31. Mary Pipher, *Reviving Ophelia: Saving the Selves of
Adolescent Girls* (New York: Ballantine Books, 1995),
57.

32. Joan Ryan, "Lost Era, Lost Illusions," *San Francisco
Sunday Examiner and Chronicle,* August 1, 1999,
Zone 7.

33. Ibid.

BIBLIOGRAPHY

Asher, Steven and Gladys Williams. "Helping Children Without Friends in Home and School Contexts." In *Children's Social Development: Information for Parents and Teachers.* Champaign/Urbana, Ill.: University of Illinois Press, 1987.

Beck, Aaron T. *Cognitive Therapy and the Emotional Disorders.* New York: New American Library, 1976.

Caen, Herb. *Baghdad by the Bay.* New York: Doubleday & Co., 1949.

Carducci, Bernardo J. *Shyness: A Bold New Approach.* New York: HarperCollins, 1999.

Chung, Connie. "Freedom Writers." *ABC News Primetime Live,* 15 April 1998, Segment #2.

Baltes, Paul B. "Longitudinal and Cross-Sectional Sequences in the Study of Age and Generation Effects." *Human Development* 11 (1968): 145–171.

Brokaw, Tom. *The Greatest Generation.* New York: Random House, 1999.

Burns, David D. *Feeling Good: The New Mood Therapy.* New York: Signet Books, 1992.

Corwin, Miles. "Mother Turns Grief, Grit to Memorial for Slain Son." *Los Angeles Times,* 29 October 1995, A27–A28.

Doherty, William. *Take Back Your Kids: Confident Parenting in Turbulent Times.* Notre Dame, Ind.: Sorin Books, 2000.

Ellis, Albert. *Reason and Emotion in Psychotherapy.* New York: Stuart, 1979.

Erikson, Erik H. *Childhood and Society.* New York: W. W. Norton & Co., 1963.

———. *Identity: Youth and Crisis.* New York: W. W. Norton & Co., 1968.

Feng, Gia-fu, and Jane English (translators). *Tao Te Ching by Lao Tsu.* New York: Random House, 1972.

Frank, Anne and B. M. Mooyaart (translator). *Anne Frank: The Diary of a Young Girl.* New York: Bantam, 1993.

Freud, Sigmund. *An Outline of Psychoanalysis.* New York: Norton & Co., 1949.

———. *Civilization and Its Discontents.* London: Hogarth Press, 1955.

Friel, John C., and Linda D. Friel. *Adult Children: The Secrets of Dysfunctional Families.* Deerfield Beach, Fla.: Health Communications, Inc., 1988.

————. *The 7 Worst Things (Good) Parents Do.* Deerfield Beach, Fla.: Health Communications, Inc., 1999.

————. *The Soul of Adulthood: Opening the Doors.* Deerfield Beach, Fla.: Health Communications, Inc., 1995.

Galinsky, Ellen. *Ask the Children: What America's Children Really Think About Working Parents.* New York: William Morrow & Co., 1999.

Ginsberg, Allen. *Howl and Other Poems.* San Francisco: City Lights Books, 1956.

Golding, William G. *Lord of the Flies.* New York: Perigee, 1959.

Goleman, Daniel. *Emotional Intelligence: Why It Can Matter More Than IQ.* New York: Bantam, 1995.

Gottman, John M. *Why Marriages Succeed or Fail.* New York: Simon & Schuster, 1994.

Gould, Roger. *Transformations: Growth and Change in Adult Life.* New York: Simon & Schuster, 1978.

Gray, Farnum, Paul S. Graubard and Harry Rosenberg. "Little Brother Is Changing You." *Psychology Today,* March 1974, 42–46.

Greenberger, Dennis, and Christine A. Padesky. *Mind over Mood: Change How You Feel by Changing the Way You Think.* New York: The Guilford Press, 1995.

Halvorsen, Donna. "Judge Faults Arrest, Drops Charges

in High-Profile Drunken-Driving Case." *Minneapolis Star Tribune,* 20 April 1995, B1.

Jeffrey, Nancy Ann. "Bratlash." *The Wall Street Journal.* Reprinted in the *Minneapolis Star Tribune,* 22 January 2000, E1–E2.

Johnson, Peter. "Secret Service Opens Up in School Shootings Report." *USA Today,* 14 March 2000.

Kantrowitz, Barbara, and Pat Wingert. "How Well Do You Know Your Kids?" *Newsweek,* 10 May 1999, 36–40.

Kaufman, Gershen. *Shame: The Power of Caring.* Cambridge: Schenkman Publishing Company, 1980.

Levinson, Daniel J. *The Seasons of a Man's Life.* New York: Alfred A. Knopf, 1978.

Lochman, John. "Social-Cognitive Processes of Severely Violent, Moderately Aggressive, and Nonaggressive Boys." *Journal of Clinical and Consulting Psychology,* 1994.

Love, Patricia, and Jo Robinson. *The Emotional Incest Syndrome: What to Do When a Parent's Love Rules Your Life.* New York: Bantam Books, 1990.

Luria, A. R. "The Directive Function of Speech in Development and Dissolution." *Word* 15 (1959): 351–352.

Maddock, James W., and Noel R. Larson. *Incestuous*

Families: An Ecological Approach to Understanding and Treatment. New York: W. W. Norton & Co., 1995.

McNeill, David. "The Development of Language." In Paul H. Mussen, ed. *Carmichael's Manual of Child Psychology.* 3d ed. New York: John Wiley & Sons, Inc., 1970.

Meichenbaum, Donald H. *The Nature and Modification of Impulsive Children: Training Impulsive Children to Talk to Themselves.* Research Report No. 23. Waterloo, Ontario, Canada: Department of Psychology, University of Waterloo, 10 April 1971.

Michener, James. *Journey.* New York: Fawcett Books, 1994.

Milgram, Stanley. "Behavioral Study of Obedience." *Journal of Personality and Social Psychology* 67 (1963): 371–378.

Miller, Alice. *For Your Own Good: Hidden Cruelty in Child-Rearing and the Roots of Violence.* New York: Farrar, Strauss, Giroux, 1983.

Miller, George A. "The Magic Number Seven, Plus or Minus Two: Some Limits on Our Capacity for Processing Information." *Psychological Review* 63 (1956): 81–97.

Mischel, Walter. "Theory and Research on the Antecedents of Self-Imposed Delay of Reward." In B. A. Maher, ed. *Progress in Experimental Personality Research.* Vol. 3. New York: Academic Press, 1966.

Napier, Augustus Y., and Carl Whitaker. *The Family*

Crucible: The Intense Experience of Family Therapy. New York: HarperCollins, 1988.

Nesselroade, John R. "Theory of Psychological States and Mood Action." In Raymond B. Cattell, ed. *Handbook of Modern Personality Study.* Chicago: Aldine Press, 1970.

Ornish, Dean. *Love and Survival: The Scientific Basis for the Healing Power of Intimacy.* New York: HarperCollins, 1998.

Petrie, A., and J. Petrie. *Mother Teresa.* Petrie Productions, 1985.

Piaget, Jean. *The Language and Thought of the Child.* New York: Harcourt Brace, 1926.

———. *The Origin of Intelligence in Children.* New York: International Universities Press, 1936.

———. *The Psychology of Intelligence.* New York: Harcourt Brace, 1950.

Pipher, Mary. *Reviving Ophelia: Saving the Selves of Adolescent Girls.* New York: Ballantine Books, 1995.

Ponton, Lynn E. *The Romance of Risk: Why Teenagers Do the Things They Do.* New York: Basic Books, 1998.

Rimm, Sylvia. *Dr. Sylvia Rimm's Smart Parenting: How to Parent So Children Will Learn.* New York: Crown Publishers, 1996.

Ryan, Joan. "Lost Era, Lost Illusions." *San Francisco Sunday Examiner and Chronicle,* August 1, 1999, Zone 7.

Schaie, K. Warner. "A General Model for the Study of Developmental Problems." *Psychological Bulletin* 64 (1965): 92–107.

Seligman, Martin E. P. *Learned Optimism: How to Change Your Mind and Your Life.* New York: Alfred A. Knopf, 1991.

Sheehy, Gail. *Passages: Predictable Crises of Adult Life.* New York: E. P. Dutton, 1974.

Shoda, Y., W. Mischel, and P. K. Peake. "Predicting Adolescent Cognitive and Self-Regulatory Competencies from Preschool Delay of Gratification." *Developmental Psychology* 26, no. 6 (1990): 978–986.

Sigafoos, Robert A., and Roger R. Easson. *Absolutely Positively Overnight! The Unofficial Corporate History of Federal Express.* Memphis, Tenn.: St. Luke's Press, 1983.

Spiegel, David J., R. Bloom, H. C. Kraemer and E. Gottheil. "Effect of Psychosocial Treatment on Survival of Patients with Metastatic Breast Cancer." *The Lancet* ii (1989): 888–891.

Steinbeck, John. *Cannery Row.* New York: Viking Press, 1945.

Tannen, Deborah. *You Just Don't Understand.* New York: Ballantine Books, 1991.

ABOUT THE AUTHORS

John C. Friel, Ph.D., and Linda D. Friel, M.A., are licensed psychologists in private practice in New Brighton, Minnesota, a suburb of St. Paul. They have three grown children, who have left the nest, and a female Labrador retriever and a male cockapoo who live at home with them. The Friels do individual, couple and family therapy, and ongoing men's and women's therapy groups. They present seminars and workshops in the United States, Canada, England and Ireland for the general public, hospitals, corporations, universities, mental health clinics and government agencies. They also conduct the Clearlife/Lifeworks Clinic in several U.S. locations. The Clinic is a gentle three-and-a-half-day process designed to help participants discover old patterns that are tripping them up in the present and to create new patterns that are healthier.

They are the best-selling authors of *Adult Children: The Secrets of Dysfunctional Families; An Adult Child's Guide to What's "Normal"; The Grown-Up Man: Heroes, Healing, Honor, Hurt, Hope; Rescuing Your Spirit; The Soul of*

Adulthood: Opening the Doors; The 7 Worst Things (Good) Parents Do and *The 7 Best Things (Smart) Teens Do.*

The Friels have been featured on or in *ABC News 20/20,* the *Oprah Winfrey Show, MSNBC, USA Today, Parents Magazine, Redbook, Child Magazine, The Dr. Toni Grant Show, Fox TV's Parent Table* and scores of other radio and television programs and newspapers.

They can be contacted at:
Friel Associates/ClearLife/Lifeworks
P.O. Box 120148
New Brighton, MN 55112-0013
phone: 651-628-0220
fax: 612-904-0340
(please note the two different area codes
for phone and fax)

Their Web site, which includes books, tapes, speaking schedules and a monthly column written by their two dogs, *Minnesota Sam and Abby,* is located at: *www.clearlife.com.*

John's parent training video, which will be called "How to Talk to Children About Difficult Things," is due for release in winter 2000 or spring 2001. Please check their Web site for further information.

The authors invite you to write to them and share your thoughts about being a teenager in the 21st century. Also, if you have ideas or suggestions for future books for or about teenagers, please feel free to write to the authors at the above address.

Notes